MSS. and other Communications, except those of an unappreciative character, should be addressed to The Editors, Corpus Christi College, Oxford.
All abuse etc., should be addressed to ITS IMMANENCE, THE ABSOLUTE, c/o The Universe, Anywhere Else.

New Series. *Special Illustrated Christmas Number, 1901.*

MIND!

A UNIQUE REVIEW OF

ANCIENT AND MODERN PHILOSOPHY.

EDITED BY

A TROGLODYTE,

With the Co-operation of THE ABSOLUTE and others.

CONTENTS.

[*Continued on next page.*

Originally published for the MIND! ASSOCIATION By
WILLIAMS AND NORGATE,
14 HENRIETTA STREET, COVENT GARDEN, LONDON;
and 7 BROAD STREET, OXFORD.
EDINBURGH AGENCY: 20 SOUTH FREDERICK STREET.
G.E. STECHERT, 9 EAST SIXTEENTH STREET, NEW YORK.
Price Four Shillings.

Reprinted by University Press of America

CONTENTS—*continued.*

MIND!

With an Introduction by
Warren E. Steinkraus

UNIVERSITY
PRESS OF
AMERICA

LANHAM • NEW YORK • LONDON

University Press of America,™ Inc.

4720 Boston Way
Lanham, MD 20706

3 Henrietta Street
London WC2E 8LU England

Printed in the United States of America

ISBN (Perfect): 0-8191-3249-7
ISBN (Cloth): 0-8191-3248-9

Originally published for the MIND! ASSOCIATION By
WILLIAMS AND NORGATE,
14 HENRIETTA STREET, COVENT GARDEN, LONDON;
and 7 BROAD STREET, OXFORD.
EDINBURGH AGENCY: 20 SOUTH FREDERICK STREET.
G.E. STECHERT, 9 EAST SIXTEENTH STREET, NEW YORK.

INTRODUCTION

The number of philosophers noted for their humor or sense of fun is remarkably small. Probably the wittiest in modern times was William James. In Ralph Perry's classic biography appear two photographs taken by James's daughter, by prearrangement, up near Mt. Chocorua in New Hampshire. The first picture shows James casually chatting with his colleague, the idealist Josiah Royce. The next, taken a few seconds later shows the dismay registered on Royce's face after James punctuated their conversation with the unexpected exclamation, "Damn the Absolute." But that sort of thing is an exception. Most philosophers in our own day are over-serious. The only British analytic philosopher with any overt sense of humor seems to have been J.L. Austin who requested that the title of his last book be a parody of Jane Austen's *Sense and Sensibility.* Now there was another book by a J. Austin, this time called *Sense and Sensibilia.* Of course, Bertrand Russell had a sharp wit and wrote many funny things. A collection of his humor and clever anecdotes would comprise a sizable volume. Few realize that Francis Herbert Bradley, unquestionably the prime figure motivating the burlesque issue of *Mind* which follows, may be credited with some quips from his notebook which he prints in the Foreword to *Appearance and Reality.* On "Optimism," Bradley wrote: "The world is the best of all possible worlds and everything in it is a necessary evil." And on "Pessimism" we read, "Where all is rotten, it is a man's work to cry stinking fish." Even Thomas Hobbes, whose clergyman-father once startled his congregation after a night of playing cards by exclaiming in a doze (while his clerk was reading) "Clubs is trumps,"—was not without some humor. He wondered why Descartes could not have said: "I walk therefore I am." Even Francis Bacon used wit to deflate the nonempirical Aristotelians. When Bacon submitted a copy of the *Novum Organum* to King James in 1620, the king noted that it was like the "peace of God which passeth all understanding."

Kant's analysis of a couple of jokes in his *Critique of Judgment,* is funnier than the jokes. An Indian seeing a bottle of ale opened expressed astonishment upon seeing the froth ooze out in such quantity. Responding to a questioner, he said: "I am not at all astonished that it should flow out, but I do wonder how you ever got it in." Says Kant:

> At this story we laugh and it gives us hearty pleasure, not because we deem ourselves cleverer than this ignorant man or because of

> anything in it that we note as satisfactory to the understanding, but because our expectation was strained (for a time) and then was suddenly dissipated into nothing.

The zealously serious Fichte, whose exact philosophical antithesis is surely George Santayana, would have been as chagrined by Santayana's crack, "There is no God and the Virgin Mary is his mother," as he would have been to see a picture of the youthful Santayana "in drag" participating in Harvard's "Hasty Pudding" show in the 1880's. It is passing strange that Santayana wrote a book in epistemology to prove by reason that "animal faith," not reason, made knowledge possible.

Except for characterizing Schelling's philosophy as "a night in which all cows are black," one finds little in Hegel that can be called funny. But Schleiermacher's definition of religion as the feeling of absolute dependence, led Hegel to quip that on that basis, a dog is the most religious being. Though he is not given to humor and has been the recipient of many cracks, most misinformed, Hegel was quite a normal human being who loved to play Whist, liked Rossini's music, and wrote love letters to his financeé after the fashion of an unphilosophical lover. At the height of his popularity, his philosophy inspired some short plays. One, written by F.W. Linder in 1844, and called "The Absolute Boot," is about a shoemaker who applies the dialectic in his trade, with some odd results. (A performance of this in translation was given at the Hegel Society meeting in 1980). A look at Feuerbach's epigrams shows that he was clever but more bitter than humorous. The temperamentally pessimistic Schopenhauer wrote brilliant sarcasm and was a paradigm of male chauvinism. The oddest thing he did, besides avoiding haircuts, was to dress up formally every day and walk his white poodle.

If we may count Voltaire a philosopher, we could claim that his wit exceeded all others. Once, when he doffed his hat as a statue of Jesus went by in a religious procession, he was asked "why" by a friend who knew he was an agnostic. Voltaire retorted: "We salute but we do not speak." He made fun of the overbearing teleological views of Christian Wolff in *Candide.* Wolff was able to find a purpose in everything. The pole star and the other stars obviously existed so man could find his way at night. And nighttime was planned so that humans could sleep or carry out pursuits not possible in daylight. To all this Voltaire scoffed: "How good it is that God created us with noses; how else should we be able to put on our spectacles!"

Berkeley's seven part dialogue, *Alciphron,* is not widely read or discussed but it is full of wit, satire and good writing. Its editor, T.E. Jessop, observes "that his style swings freely from solemnity to levity, holding and communicating every mood except the tragic . . . . We are never far from a big vision or a piece of vivid wit." But *Alciphron* pokes fun at free-thinkers, elite intellectuals and self-styled critics of honest religion. It reflects the biting wit of Berkeley's close friend, Jonathan Swift. Where else could one read:

> And the man of raillery who would as soon bite off his tongue as break a jest on the profession of arms in the presence of a military man, shall instantly brighten up and assume a familiar air with religion and the church before ecclesiastics.

Berkeley's attack on those he called "minute philosophers" could be updated in an effort to deflate some of the tedious discussions of contemporary philosophers and uninformed critics of genuine religion.

Henri Bergson is one of the few philosophers who tried to analyze the comic philosophically. In his intriguing essay called *Laughter,* he tells the story of a man who was asked why he did not weep at a sermon while everyone else who heard it was shedding tears. The reply was, "I don't belong to the parish." Bergson's point is that humor usually is affiliated with some social group and refers to a set of customs and ideas. Laughter "implies a kind of secret free-masonry, or even complicity with other laughers." Indeed, one must have some feeling and kinship for the philosophical tradition if one is to "get" philosophical humor. Accordingly, Josiah Royce could occasionally provoke a prominent smile, if not laughter, among those acquainted with his viewpoint and that of his colleague William James. In his *Philosophy of Loyalty,* Royce tried to imagine what it would be like for a pragmatist like James to take the witness stand in a courtroom. Because of his conscientious scruples and his fine new definition of truth in terms of which alone he could be sworn in, the pragmatist would have to say something like this: "I promise to tell whatever is expedient and nothing but what is expedient, so help me future experience."

Another of William James' friends, Borden P. Bowne, wrote some of the wittiest sarcasm to be found anywhere in American philosophy. In ridiculing David Strauss's book *The Old Faith and the New,* back in 1874, Bowne wrote: "The amount of talent necessary to construct this argument is not remarkably great, but the amount required to believe it borders on the supernatural." Later: "The limits of absurdity have not only been reached, but transcended." Such jeers did not make Bowne popular but they are funny. Once, Professor John Tyndall, a British physicist, proposed that religious beliefs could be subjected to testing by experimenting with the sick in a hospital. The idea was that prayers should be said for patients in one ward but not for those in another. After a time the results could be compared and the alleged benefits of prayer be evaluated. Bowne wrote an answer in 1877, called "The Prayer Test Improved." He recommended that some remote tribe in Central Africa be presented systematically with the latest truths of advanced science and be carefully guarded from pernicious religious doctrines. Under such circumstances the best results would be achieved "and humanity after ages of thwarting and baffling error would at last reach truth and would bud and blossom as a rose."

While not many philosophers write with tongue in cheek, or with foot in pocket, for that matter, some have occasionally done or said notably funny things. Rousseau once threw his watch away saying, "Thank heaven, I shall no longer find it necessary to know what time of the day it is." And Hume, who didn't like Rousseau's character at all, once wrote a friend saying he wanted a room "in a sober, discreet family, who would not be averse to admit a sober, discreet and virtuous, regular quiet good-natured man of bad character." Jeremy Bentham left his entire estate to the University of London with the proviso that his embalmed remains be present at all subsequent meetings of the Board. Accordingly, the stuffed and clothed skeleton of Bentham, seated in a transportable cabinet, may still be seen at that university on certain occasions.

In 1865, J. Hutchison Stirling wrote a two volume treatise to reveal *The Secret of Hegel,*—but everybody said he kept it. Ralph Barton Perry once characterized a group of his contemporaries as thinkers who had "sold their philosophical birthright for a mess of positivism." William James loved to play with double meanings. He noted that when one heard someone speak of the need for "a more monistic philosophy, it could also be taken to mean 'a Mormonistic philosophy'." If one reads aloud, noted James, the visually meaningless French words "*pas de leur Rhône que nous*," one sees that it really says, "Paddle your own canoe."

Brand Blanshard reports on the antics of C.E.M. Joad, who was productive philosophically and a regular on the B.B.C. He was a practical joker *à toute outrance.* As a house guest one time, he carried some Brussells sprouts in his pocket from the luncheon table up to a nursery "to secrete them inside a child's rocking-horse, producing soon a stench whose source it was almost impossible to locate." In travelling back and forth to London, it amused Joad, by changing cars and other means, to outwit the Great Western Railway and pay no fares. But detectives learned of this and watched him. His game as well as his public career was ended in a magistrate's court with a stiff fine.

Surely the funniest philosopher in recent years was the late Harry Costello, who, incidentally, was Bertrand Russell's assistant at Harvard in 1914. His friends say he sported a puckish sense of humor and an editor remarked that his book notices "though mischievous in tone were deliberate and penetrating." Among other things, Costello's little book, *A Philosophy of the Real and the Possible* (1954) contains a high proportion of comic anecdotes and witticisms. Sartre's Existentialism is characterized as the "philosophy of the frustrated will, that cold grey dawn in which all cows are purple." Whitehead is described as a little man "a bit roly-poly with a cheerful face" who reminded Costello "of a kewpie doll." Linguistic behaviorists illustrated "a Mickey Mouse stage, behavior plus squeaks." He saw Hegelianism as "that lion's cave where all the other animal tracks lead inwards but none come out again." One of his favorite rimes was,

> I am Francis Herbert Bradley
> When my liver acts up badly,
> I take refuge from the brute
> In the blessed Absolute.

Costello reports that a teacher committed to John Dewey's method was asked by a young pupil: "Teacher, do we have to do just what we want to all day long?" He reported the crack that whenever a new thought came to Bertrand Russell. Russell believed it was a new discovery of the human race.

Of course, there is no reason why Philosophy should be any funnier than Chemistry or Astronomy. And there is no basis for presuming that philosophers should behave in funnier ways than scientists. But maybe those seventeen or eighteen people who zealously want to make philosophy into an "exact" discipline, or those twenty-three who view it as a branch of science, would be happier if they punctured some of their over-intense concerns with some appropriate wit. Someone might also seek to penetrate the deadly serious world of the modern logician with all of his "such thats," "if and only ifs" and "I know that p's." A good contemporary parody would be salutary for modern British and North American analysts with their "putative analyticities" and "illocutionary utterances." And who can estimate the health-giving power of a good burlesque on overconfident Marxist-Leninists or on the wistful hermeneutical divagations of Continental philosophy? If one would attempt Heidegger in rime or poke fun at some of Kierkegaard's learned froth, he would no doubt be treated as a burnable heretic. "Born again" Existentialists or Wittgensteinians are like my Freudian friend who told me once that all of Freud's critics were "mentally ill." That's not much better than arguing that the first thing Satan does is to get you to doubt his existence.

A parody of *Nous,* or *Analysis* or even the *Journal of Philosophy* would surely irritate the over-serious dedication of those bright young analytic philosophers, but its deflationary value would be worth it. They remind one of the piano virtuoso who has mastered Liszt, let us say, and is sure there is no other music, mostly because he has neither heard or studied it. And what great benefit would accrue from some jibes against the gushes of those Ivy League philosophers who have worked out ingenious "logical" defenses of American greed and who contemplate favorably moribund right-wing political views?

The verbal antics of those who parade minute logical distinctions, as if that were all there is to philosophy, are a wonder to behold. But if one views such displays, particularly when presented orally, as entertainment rather than as wisdom, he can occasionally find something of value. It is surprising how you can fool a dedicatee of this stuff if you put together a string of jargon with a note of seriousness. I tried it once, and a friend who was in the know, burst out laughing at the intent posture of my eager subject who was hanging on every word of my pure jibberish because it *sounded* like it might have meant something. We are slowly getting away from that homogeneity of erudition which has characterized so many younger philosophers who are afraid to think for themselves and behave towards their sometimes haughty mentors like some lowly, quivering German "assistant" before his "doctor-father." Nevertheless, one could still write a short essay on how to succeed in philosophy without doing anything more than emitting certain acceptable sounds. Just as Shaw's *Pygmalion* shows what can be done by a steady but superficial training of one's manner of speaking, so it seems highly probable that philosophic froth and foam can be cleverly concealed by those who are well-trained in the current philosophical patter. One needs only to recall the horror with which the British philosophic establishment greeted Gellner's exposé of Wittgenstein some years ago. Bertrand Russell loved it and wrote an Introduction. But Gilbert Ryle refused to have it reviewed in *Mind*. It is still on the analysts' *Index Expurgatorius* as is Marcuse's comparable unmasking of "One Dimensional Philosophy."

There have been two recent attempts to approach Philosophy from a humorous standpoint. In 1972, James Taylor published *A Porcine History of Philosophy and Religion.* This consists of fifty cartoons depicting pigs in such poses as: "A follower of Democritus immediately after consuming a quantity of particularly smooth atoms," a "Kantian pig prior to awaking from his dogmatic slumber," and "Two Sartrian pigs in the days of resistance." Very recently, Richard Aquila has assembled four hundred limericks to characterize philosophical views in his *Rhyme or Reason: A Limerick History of Philosophy* (1981). But the "classical" effort at philosophical humor in the Western World is the parody on *Mind* which follows.

We do not know much about the actual background of this striking publication nor who all the contributors were, but we do know something about Ferdinand Canning Scott Schiller, its editor and the likely source for most of the material. Schiller was born in Schleswig-Holstein in 1864, studied at Rugby and Oxford, there receiving the M.A. From 1893 to 1897, he was at Cornell University as an instructor and graduate student under J.E. Creighton. His *Riddles of the Sphinx* (London: 1891) was submitted for the doctorate but was not accepted. Schiller returned to

Corpus Christi College in Oxford. In 1901, he became treasurer of the Mind Association. He published a number of books, but his best known are *Humanism* (1903) and *Studies in Humanism* (1907). He was President of the Aristotelian Society in 1921, and became a member of the British Academy in 1926. He began as a visiting lecturer at the University of Southern California that year, finally taking up permanent residence there in 1935. He died in 1937.

In 1902, he published a somewhat whimsical article in *Mind* called "Useless Knowledge: A Discourse Concerning Pragmatism." In the same year, an important article "Axioms and Postulates" appeared in a collection of essays edited by Henry Sturt called *Personal Idealism.* Here Schiller held that the laws of thought are not principles of being or rules of logic but simply postulates. This essay contained a funny bit about Kant. It was no doubt written at the time Schiller was preparing the burlesque edition of *Mind.* He writes:

> Personally I have long felt towards the Kantian epistemology not much otherwise than Alphonso the Wise felt towards the Ptolemaic Astronomy when he realized its growing complications; and if by incantations or recantations or decantations I could induce its author to leave the society and *otium cum dignitate* of the Thing-in-itself, I would fain relieve my feelings by apostrophising him as follows: 'Oh mighty Master of both worlds and both reasons, Thinker of Noumena, and Seer of Phenomena, Schematiser of Categories, Contemplator of the Pure Forms of Intuition, Unique Synthesizer of Apperceptions, Sustainer of all Antinomies, all-pulverising Annihilator of Theoretic Gods and Rational Psychologies, I conjure thee by these or by whatever other titles thou hast earned the undying gratitude of countless commentators, couldst thou not have constructed a theory of our thinking activity more lucidly and more simply?' (p.78f)

Schiller called his philosophy "Humanism" in order to point out the dependence of knowledge and truth on human nature and on the religious and moral demands of the person. His emphasis on the concrete individual person gave him a certain affinity with Personalism but he was viewed by some as a modern follower of Protagoras. He was an inveterate foe of Absolute Idealism, and particularly of F.H. Bradley. He actually viewed the latter's philosophy as "inhuman, incompetent and impracticable intellectualism." When one recalls that Schiller took the view that truth claims may be made in *jokes,* as well as in postulates, assumptions, fiction and even lies, it is easier to see his aim in producing *Mind*!. What better way to put down Absolute Idealism than by making fun of it!

In 1907, there was a student review played by Oxford youths called "The Old Man of Königsberg." It parodied the debate between monistic and pluralistic philosophers with "the man who monises" and "the man who prgamatises." It is beyond belief to think that Schiller was not involved in this enterprise. In the same year, he had an article in the *Journal of Philosophy* called "A Pragmatic Babe in the Woods" which prints some doggerel about monists and pluralists. His pragmatic opposition to Absolute Idealism may have reflected despair in understanding; it also served to deflate pomposity. And that is always valuable. Socrates did it too. In the *Theaetetus,* he is criticized for "running" Protagoras too hard. He replied: "But it is not clear that we are outrunning the truth, my friend." (171)

Schiller's *Riddles of the Sphinx,* which went through three editions, the last in 1910, was published under the pseudonym A. Troglodyte. He used the selfsame pseudonym as editor of *Mind!.* "Troglodyte" is from the Greek and means "one who creeps into holes," and has come to mean not only one of any savage race that dwells in caves but also any person of primitive and degraded ways of living. It is, consequently, not hard to see why Schiller's biographer, Reuben Abel, said that Schiller maintained the role of "philosophic *enfant terrible*."

Mind! was issued in 1901 as a Christmas number. There is no reference to it any place in the regular copies of *Mind,* either for the preceding year or for two years afterwards. It was not included in any subscription fee. But it was referred to in *Mind* at least once, in the 1950 volume, when a small advertisement appeared on p. 431. This was an ad noting the discovery of "a considerable parcel of undistributed copies" which the publisher, Thomas Nelson & Sons, was prepared to dispose of at two shillings sixpence. The advertisement read: "This did not of course belong to the *Mind* series, though it was got up to look like numbers of this series." Further, this notice confirms that this burlesque issue was produced by F.C.S. Schiller, with some help, "under the pseudonym of A. Troglodyte."

The scholarly apparatus necessary to clarify *all* the allusions and citations in the magazine would probably require a collection of notes almost as long as the original. The erudition and subtlety of the editor are broad-ranging. Several languages are used. It is not obvious that today's readers would be served if the sundry footnotes were translated, but they too are quite funny. If one remembers that the chief object of disrespect is the Absolute, from the frontispiece onward, and that all philosophers of any prominence in both Europe and the United States who were sympathetic to Idealism are recipients of Schiller's attacks, he may be helped in detecting the allusions. We will call attention to a few: J.E.M. Tagrag (p. 131) is J.M.E. MacTaggart who wrote two books on Hegel and developed a system of non-theistic Absolute Idealism. "Grin" refers to Thomas Hill Green (1836-1882), an idealistic critic of Hume and predecessor of Schiller at Oxford. "Cared" can refer to either of the two Caird brothers, Edward or John, Scottish Hegelians. "Joyce" is certainly Royce (p. 137).

"Crichton" is no doubt J.E. Creighton, the Cornell Idealist who was chairman of the department at the time Schiller tried unsuccessfully for the Ph.D. J.H. Stirling, mentioned above, is meant (p. 138). Mary Whiton Calkins (p. 11), a Wellesley philosophy professor who combined Royce's Absolutism with Personalism, is the only woman philosopher referred to. George Trumbull Ladd, the Yale Idealist, is the person intended in verse #87 (p. 108). On page 106, there is a citation to Henry Sturt, an editor of a volume cited previously. The German Idealists are repeatedly cited. Kant comes in for a share of the fun as well with "The Critique of Pure Rot."

Other names that may not be immediately recognized are Paul Carus (p. 64 & #88 on p. 109), founder and first editor of *The Monist,* G.F. Stout (p. 106) an editor of *Mind.* There is a reference to Samuel Alexander, the Australian and British Neo-Realist who wrote the important book *Space, Time and Deity* (p. 107), and there is a citation to A.M. Fairbairn, a prominent philosophical theologian of the period (p. 140). The influential opponent of Hegel, J.F. Herbart is mentioned (p. 75). Bywater is a translator of early Greek philosophers and James Baldwin was editor of the first *Dictionary of Philosophy and Psychology.* "Biljames" is certainly William James (p. 137) And Carveth Read was a reviewer for *Mind* who later wrote *The Origin of Man and His Superstitions* (1920) which maintains that human culture is all due to the results of a flesh diet and the consequent hunter's life.

In addition, there are some relatively obscure allusions to local Oxford traditions and customs (e.g. p. 119) which would require the sort of research *Mind!* does not deserve. Esoteric Greek passages and footnotes seem as apparently as strained and funny as the Latin and German ones are. The hymn cited on page 14, may be sung to the tune of "Come Thou Almighty King" by Felice de Giardini.

Readers will recognize allusions to all sorts of things that flitted through Schiller's fertile imagination. The myth about Empedocles jumping into Aetna's volcano (p. 134) is based on the poem by Matthew Arnold. And the "Tree of Porphyry" refers to something quite other than that intended by that fourth century thinker. Readers will often be reminded of the American humorist Ogden Nash, especially when they see such things as "X.N. O'Fun" for Xenophon (p. 132). *Ursus Spelaeus* (p. 60) means bear cave. That may be the possible dwelling place of A. Troglodyte himself. Or, maybe the manuscript for *Mind!* was indeed found in the belly of a crocodile of literary taste! (p. 32)

January 1983

Warren E. Steinkraus
Department of Philosophy
SUNY-Oswego
Oswego, New York

This side up.

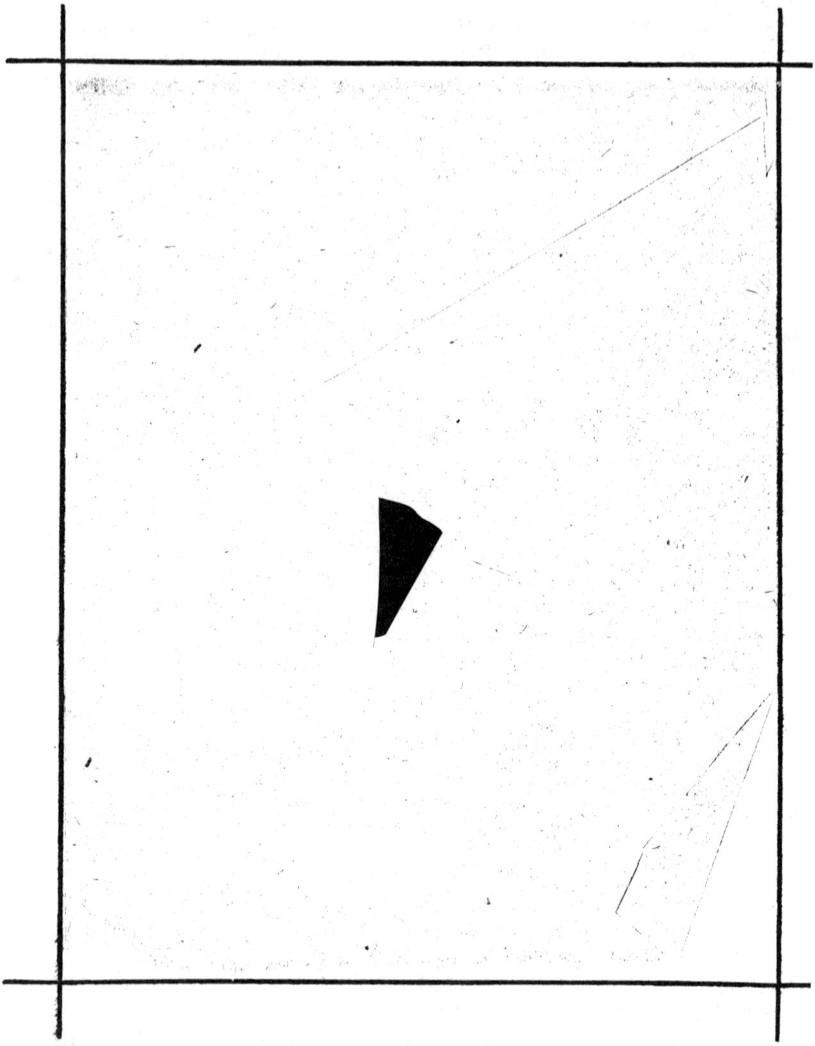

PORTRAIT OF ITS IMMANENCE THE ABSOLUTE.

Instructions for Use.—Turn the eye of faith, fondly but firmly, on the centre of the page, wink the other, and gaze fixedly until you see It.

I.—FRONTISPIECE.

It is with the utmost satisfaction that we present to our readers an *authentic Portrait* of the Absolute, in full panoply, R-rayed in the parinfernalia of Its Office and X-rayed by the new and powerful *Shamoscope* which we have recently invented and patented and can warrant to see through everything. On (pink [1]) paper the result looks surprisingly simple, and very like the Bellman's map in the *Hunting of the Snark.* But in reality it was a difficult achievement. We realised from the first that Mind! could, as little as anything else, be complete without the Absolute, and determined to use It as an illustration regardless of the expense of the most abstruse and occult processes.

So we advertised for representative *Aspects* of the Absolute, thinking to compile therefrom a composite photo which should be an absolutely authentic image of the Absolute. They came in shoals, Doctors, Pholisophers of every description, and all Its valiant supporters. But when our *modus operandi* was explained to them a terrific tumult arose. Each declared that the rest were phenomenal impostors, and that he alone was adequate to represent the Whole. There is no saying what would have happened, but for the presence of Mind! shown by our Office Boy. He chanced to be entertaining himself with blowing bubbles from a large basin of soap and water. Some he dispersed in pursuit of bubbles, which they hastily identified with the Absolute, others by the direr menace of a scrubbing brush and of the contents of his basin. Shortly afterwards the invention of the *Shamoscope* offered a welcome means of avoiding all such difficulties and of producing a portrait, which, we trust, will prove equally satisfactory to those who admire the Absolute and to those who do not. All who have seen It assure us that it is an excellent likeness.

[1] It is, of course, the pink of Perfection.

II.—EDITORIAL.

"Now all things were mixed; then MIND! came and set all things in order."—ANAXAGORAS.

THE appearance of a "*Nova*" in the intellectual sky is apt to attract attention and demand explanation. We therefore hasten to assure the public that no harm is intended, and that MIND! is not meant to compete *seriously* with the already too numerous existing journals of philosophy. Its aim is rather to relieve than to enhance the existing depression of Philosophy, by throwing light on an aspect of Experience which philosophers have too often and too long neglected.

Philosophic depression, indeed, is no novelty. Like its agricultural congener, it may be traced back by the leisured and learned to the very earliest records of human effort. Already in a papyrus of the First Dynasty Dul-prig-bah, the worthy Hierophant of the Ineffable Mysteries, attached to the shrine of *Pooh* at Memphis, complains that the young are no longer eager—as in the days of his youth—to throng to philosophic discourses (his own) and prefer to chase the hippopotami upon the sacred river. Perhaps such complaints are like those of the degeneracy of the stage and the turf, and of the decay in the arts of conversation and of being polite to bores, and mean no more.

In case, however, that there should be a substratum of truth in them, it seems worth while to try a novel remedy. Hence the appearance of MIND! the levity and flippancy of which must be regarded as part of a deep-laid plot to inculcate into its readers philosophic gravity and enthusiasm. For it is a well-known psychological law that the dreams of metaphysicians also act by contraries, especially upon the young and intelligent.

Again, owing to the growth of amenities in criticism it has become almost impossible to speak the Truth, *nisi ridentem dicere verum*, and the deity whom so many profess ignorantly to worship is reluctantly compelled to array herself in motley.

We have aimed therefore, primarily and conscientiously, at fun, and if occasionally our shafts may seem to the supersensitive to have been somewhat too sharply pointed, the benignant reader who enters into the spirit of our enterprise will, we trust, kindly put this down to the necessity of hitting wisdom, before she flies off into those regions of the supra-sensible whence there is no return. It is the fault also of the subject if we have not always overcome the proverbial difficulty of not writing satire, and at all events we may claim that there was not an ounce of malice in our fun. As to this the subjoined report of the famous geloiologist, Dr. Joe King, Ph.D., F.R.S., F.G.S., F.C.S., etc., bears gratifying testimony :—

"The jocoscopic analysis of the light of the '*Nova Mentis*, 1901,' shows a pretty continuous bright spectrum chiefly composed of the 'enhanced' lines due to the presence of large quantities of the more frivolous gases. This is an indication of extremely genial warmth, which is confirmed by the fact that even the most refractory solids appear to have been volatilised, and to shine by their own light. The most delicate instruments however failed to show any dark lines (even in the poetry) due to malice. The cause therefore of the phenomenon remains obscure. It would be premature to decide whether it arose from the spontaneous combustion of a hitherto unobserved philosophic luminary, or was due to a collision of academic wits. Nevertheless I feel it my duty to state that I consider it a *very grave* phenomenon, as indicating serious and incalculable convulsions in the unintelligible world and perhaps heralding the end of an epoch in philosophic history."

Nothing could be more reassuring than this report.

We may also console ourselves with the thought that whatever the character of our ridicule, ridicule does not kill, and least of all the immortals; to whom it will be noticed that we have restricted our impertinences. If therefore any rumour thereof should penetrate to the lucid intervals amid the whirl of worlds, they will doubtless appreciate the real compliment which lurks beneath our ostensible liberties. As for their adherents, they should remember the excellent maxim of the tolerant Emperor, *deorum injuriæ dis curæ*.

In conclusion a few words may be added on the title we have chosen. Like everything that is really profound, it may be explained in several divergent ways. Symbolically, MIND! admonishes to the caution for which philosophers are justly renowned. Historically, it revives the almost forgotten memory of the oldest philosophic journal in the world. For when the mystery of existence first began to weigh upon the palæolithic Troglodytes, *Whywhy* the Radical (whose tragic career Mr. Andrew Lang has narrated with his wonted felicity) started an advanced periodical, from which his tribe subsequently took the name of "Cave-dwellers". He called it *Cave!* and the traditional connexion between the Cave and Philosophy has been worthily maintained in well-known writings of Plato and Bacon. Now even a mediocre knowledge of Proto-Aryan speech will convince our readers that the most obvious and elegant translation of *Cave!* is *Mind!* On the ethical significance of MIND! we have descanted in our "Answers to Correspondents" (p. 141). Psychophysiologically, it reveals the hidden meaning of the maxim, "*Mens! sana in Corpore*". Most loftily it may be said, *sub specie æternitatis et rosa*, that, regarded in its true inwardness and metaphysical Essence, MIND! is the primordial source of the Rejuvenescence of Philosophy, and so *Eternal*, while all its terrestrial copies emanate from and adumbrate this archetypal exemplar, in which they are immanent. And lastly, and confidentially, to all philosophers, of whatsoever creed and breed, we seek in our title to convey the much-needed warning that a sense of humour is the salvation of a true Sanity of Mind!

III.—THE PLACE OF HUMOUR IN THE ABSOLUTE.

By F. H. Badly.

Introductory Note.

[This chapter somehow got omitted from my famous work on the *Disappearance of Reality*—perhaps because the Editor of *Punch* failed to return it in time for me to include it. As however that work—which only the fatuous ignorance of prejudiced ineptitude could have pronounced a philosophic hoax—did not profess to be systematic, I dare say the great majority of my readers never noticed the omission. I now publish it, not so much because I flatter myself that the English mind is capable of the strenuous effort of attention requisite for really understanding it, or because I think that metaphysicians are too much in earnest with metaphysics, and as the phrase runs take themselves too seriously, but merely to show that dogmatic pedantry no longer occupies the whole ground as the one accredited way of "philosophic thinking".

The paper of course speaks for itself, and I might leave it to do so, but now that I have gone so far in taking my readers (if any) into my confidence (such as it is), I find myself unable to refrain from transcribing some sentences from a dusty old notebook which I happened to light upon lately—compiled, apparently, while I was circumventing the examiners for the dreary, and now happily extinct, farce humorously called 'the Rudiments of Faith and Religion'!

"Metaphysics," I there find written, "is no joke—until you come to write it—and then the joke soon ceases when you are asked to explain what you have written."

Of Religion I have said, "it is the funniest thing in the world—until you come to believe it; and then you fail to see the fun of it any longer and become the funniest thing yourself"; of the religious, "of all those who take life religiously the *Thug* is the least noxious".

About the Unity of the Universe I have set down the paradox that "the *One* always means *a great many things*":

about the Many, that "the more you have of them, the more you want the One".

Concerning Truth and Falsehood I lay it down that "it is all one, and God knows the difference; if he knows anything": concerning Good and Evil, that "they differ only in the time it takes to see through them: but it is good not to do so too soon, and evil to do so before you are in a position to do it with impunity".

Similarly I declare that "Time is unreal, but it takes most people some time to realise this," while about Space I feel that "it is strange that I am at its centre everywhere and its circumference nowhere".

As for Telepathy, I admit that "there are many minds worth reading—especially on the Stock Exchange".

Of vocal Pessimism I remark that "to cry *stinking fish* is folly: when your nose is offended, you had much better keep your mouth shut".

Lastly I discover that "to love satisfied the world is a nuisance, to love unsatisfied a hindrance; but to love or not to love *that* is the question".

The reader may judge (though I doubt it) how far these dicta form sense, and he must please himself also how seriously he takes them. *Me* assuredly he can *not* please, and so I will say no more.—F. H. B.]

My attitude towards my Absolute has struck many as a pleasantry, the point of which lies in its consciousness. It has seemed a proposal to take something for God simply and solely because I *know* I don't know what the devil it can be. It is, however, a mere misunderstanding (the removal of which is not properly my concern) to attribute to me such an extreme of ingenuity. I have really no wish to be irreverent, and can content myself with saying that to the untutored human mind the Absolute is distinctly humorous. It may come from a failure in my metaphysics, or from an exuberance of the flesh which continues to distract me, but the notion that there should be no place for Humour in the Absolute strikes as cold and desiccating as the dreariest dogmatism. That the fun of this world in the end is appearance, leaves the world funnier, if we feel it is a symbol of some diviner merriment; but the phenomenal jest is a deception and a cheat, if it hides some grim travesty of our hopes, some veiled horror of unlaughable enigma, some noümenal *cancan* of a bloodthirsty monster. Though dragged to such entertainments one cannot enjoy them—any more than an Oxford garden party.

Fortunately, however, I have already more than once picturesquely and unequivocally asserted that the Absolute is the reality which includes, unites, immerses, over-rides, overpowers, owns, swallows, absorbs, transmutes, transfigures and transcends all appearances.

With such an Absolute one is safe. Without it there would be no fun in metaphysics. All the fun, therefore, must be within it. Once, therefore, he has grasped it, firmly, by the scruff of the neck, even the most benighted idiot among my readers[1] can hardly fail to see that, like everything else, humour must be contained in the Absolute.

It is no use standing aghast, therefore, at the atrocity of some of the puns which will doubtless be perpetrated by others of the contributors to this journal, nor urging against the obscurity of others that there are some jokes no man can comprehend. If you cannot comprehend the joke, that only proves that the joke is *beyond you*, not that it is *beyond the Absolute*, which must be supposed to be adequate to the comprehension of the Infinite Jest whereof we all are parts. We must subside therefore and allow the Absolute to absorb all its appearances, jokes and all.

It would be easy, if one took the trouble, to prove in another way that the Absolute must take in jokes, without being taken in itself—although we may be. We can not therefore regard the Absolute with levity, but must preserve our gravity in discussions of the sort. For if we lost it, where should we be? Not in the universe, assuredly; for gravitation is universal. And to be levitated into a spirit world beyond the Absolute is impossible. For there is no spirit world, and if there were, it would be within the Absolute and therefore Appearance. For the Absolute is the absolute centre of gravity of the universe and the universe is one, one with the Absolute. Whoever denies or doubts this should be condemned to recite my Postulate 10,000 times before breakfast.

'But appearances,' you say, 'are against the Absolute.' What of that? How could they be anything else? And where would the fun come in if they were not? But they are only appearances, and hardly worth preserving. For the

[1] [Isn't this rather too rude even from you, Mr. B.? One knows, of course, that you don't mean all these sayings to be taken too seriously, but they give you such a false air of arrogance, which distresses the weaker brethren.—ED., MIND! Had no intention to be rude, but felt they must be idiots to read me. I'm an extra-humble-minded man really.—F. H. B. No doubt; but are you not a good deal more humble-minded about your readers?—ED., MIND! Appearance.—F. H. B.]

Absolute is bound to swallow them, or any other nonsense it may please any one to propound, if we cannot. But you 'do not see how the Absolute can digest such jests'. It is not necessary that you should; it is enough that the Absolute should swallow them, and dissolve what it swallows into the fuller harmony of its internal economy.

Not of course that it is necessary to affirm that the ideal content of a joke, *recognised as such*, must be referred to a Reality beyond a joke, which is the Absolute. No one of the great philosophers, who have declined to consort with malingering chimeras like God, Freedom and Immortality, has ever asserted anything of the kind.[1] And *I*, of course, do not wish to be peculiar and to stand alone.

So I will simply state, quite abruptly, that the Absolute, whatever it may be in relation to the Universe, is not humorous as such and in itself (*An und für Sich*)—for the simple reason that *it has absolutely no sense of humour*. How indeed could it, seeing that it has absolutely no sense of any kind? The senses are appearance and deceptive to boot, while the Absolute is Reality, and has never had the audacity to deceive me. Moreover the Absolute is Experience and rather a terrible experience at that, and no joke.

Do I, in so saying, contradict my previous assertion that the Absolute is humorous? Not at all. I am not a Hegelian, though I have never concealed my approbation of Hegel, and still cannot help thinking that if Hegel's *Phänomenologie* were substituted for Latin Prose in Smalls, and his *Greater Logic* for Mill in Honour Mods, Merton would be much quieter, and perhaps even a possible college to inhabit in term time, while the English mind would get a real chance of becoming truly philosophic.

But I have always retained a, perhaps exaggerated, regard for the Principle of Contradiction, so that nothing pleases me more than to see it outraged by others. (This again may be weakness of the flesh, as explained above.)

But in reality there is no such difficulty here. For all that I now say is that there is no place in the Absolute for humour *recognised as such*. It finds its place in the systematic Unity of Reality, like everything else. But it is there as *Fact*, not

[1] I give no references, partly on principle—seeing that it is always possible that some one *might* look them up and detect either one's defalcations or one's misrepresentations—partly because I am always trying to write down to the level of my readers, and it would not help them much to learn my relation to German writers whom they have not read. And even if they should read, nothing I could say would make them understand.

as *Meaning*. *I.e.*, it is *as such* suppressed,[1] transformed, transmuted, transmogrified, or in a word, transmuddled. The Absolute absorbs it together with all other appearances. Indeed it lives on them, and on nothing else. The Absolute has no food but appearances and without them would starve. And yet with appearances alone to digest, it would remain unsatisfied. It takes in everything[2] and excretes nothing.

As food stuffs, therefore, all appearances are worthless, apart from transmutation. Transubstantiation is, of course, a theological monster, but transmutation is the ultimate process which infallibly converts appearances into reality. Not that all appearances, even so, are of equal value: there are degrees, and the nutritiousness of an appearance depends on the *amount* of transmutation needed and the *time* required to effect it.[3]

But to resume: the Absolute, as in duty bound, transmutes the appearance of humour. 'Into what?' Into reality! Yah, ask another! 'How?' That tedious question again! How often am I to explain that though I cannot precisely say how, it *must* be *somehow?* And I defy any one to convince me that the trick is impossible. Have I not stated over and over again that "What can be and must be that *therefore* is"?[4] Indeed I have dwelt so often on this that I really must consider it disposed of.

What more? Why nothing! No writer who is determined to respect himself (if not others) can be called on to treat this subject seriously at greater length. Not but what I might

[1] Even the psychologists agree with us here. They tell us that suppressed laughter is still laughter, and not less laughter but more laughter. I have often verified this myself, in my youth, in church, while listening to sermons.

[2] [Except, of course, Mr. Badly himself, *v.* above.—ED., MIND!]

[3] [This is most interesting, Mr. Badly, but how does it agree with what you say elsewhere about the unreality of Time and the illusoriness of the categories of Appearance?—ED., MIND! Don't be impertinent, sir! —F. H. B.]

[4] Owing to the abysmal stupidity of my critics it is not perhaps superfluous to add that this is *not* to be taken *seriously* as a postulate. Postulates belong to a Voluntarism which I detest, and have over and over again exploded audibly. And any one capable of prostituting his intellect by resorting to postulation, will inevitably be led on to assign practical value to theoretical truth, and end as the degraded hireling of an effete priestcraft. Nothing that I choose to say, therefore, must be interpreted as an expression of and excuse for, a discreditable superstition. The way some people, who *ought* to be enlightened, talk is enough to make one whirl round and round in one's cage, like an infuriated squirrel! But there, I will be calm, if I cannot be polite!

go on for another 600 pages in this style. (My style is excellent.) But it would all come to the same thing, *viz.*, the Absolute, and I really cannot be expected to write it all out. So all I can say is—'Go to bed and sleep it off, if you can! Above all don't worry yourselves, or (what is more important) me!'

IV.—THE ESSENCE OF REALITY.

BY T. H. GRIN (*née* DE ROUGEMONT).

[The history of this article is somewhat curious. It was originally sent to our esteemed contemporary *Mind* by the most serious-minded idealist in America, who mentioned that she regarded it as the profoundest expression of the deepest convictions she had yet attained to. The Editor of *Mind* did not think it suitable, but showed it to us. We at once cabled over to the author, offering to publish it in MIND ! and to pay her fifty dollars, on condition that two or three phrases were changed. The author readily accepted these conditions and the dollars, but was very anxious that her name should appear. It was only with great difficulty that she was prevailed on to respect the rule of pseudonymity which has been adopted for MIND !, and it is respect for the same principle which prevents us also from revealing it. Nevertheless, we hope that the result will be satisfactory, and that to a careful student the article will appear in no wise unworthy to be included in the pages of MIND !—ED.]

IT is in vain that we seek to define the real by finding, either in the work of the mind or elsewhere, an unreal to which it may be opposed. For, to say of any object that it is unreal is the same as saying that there is no such thing as that object: in other words, there is no such thing as an unreal object. Of two alternatives, one. Either, as regards any particular belief, we are not mistaken at all, in which case nothing more need be said; or else we are *really* mistaken, in which case what more can we possibly want? When a quill-driver in the Schools 'makes a howler,' as we say, his addle-pated answer has its own reality just as much as if he had answered aright. There are relations between certain printed matter on the one side and his cerebral organ on the other, between the present state of the latter and certain determining conditions—whether spiritual in themselves or spirituous, we need not now stop to inquire—between the immediate sensible effect of the printed question and the mental muddle which it in turn excites, as full and definite as in any case of a correct answer. There is as much reality in the one case as in the other, but it is not the same reality. The illusion under which the candidate labours is real, not indeed with the particular reality which the subject of the illusion fondly ascribes to it, but with a reality which the superior intelligence of the examiner all too readily understands. To sum up, we do undoubtedly often take what is really related in one way to be really related in another. But this is not a confusion of the real with the unreal: it is a confusion of one particular reality with another. Mere untutored common sense is apt to lay undue stress on the fact that, of any two such realities, the one, namely the object as it really is, *ex hypothesi,* does not exist *for us*, and cannot therefore by us be confounded with anything else; whilst the other, or the object as it exists for us, is the object as it really isn't. But this consideration, which on a superficial view might seem to militate against our theory of the identity of thought with reality, does, when rightly understood, but lend additional confirmation thereto. For the consideration in question goes to show that our theory is confused as regards its treatment of error; and since it is impossible to set up an intelligible distinction between consciousness and its object, it follows of strict necessity that in treating of confusion of thought our own thought must be confused. And it is clear that the greater the confusion, the more confoundedly real must the object be.

What we have so far sought to show has been (1) generally, that any distinction between the real and the unreal is necessarily an unreal distinction, since non-existent things simply do not exist; and (2) specially, that the antithesis between reality and illusion is wholly illusory, since an illusion is as real as anything else.

We will now proceed to show that an illusion is *more* real than anything else. An object which does not exist *for us* is for us as good as nothing: and hence, plainly, it is for us that objects exist. That is, the reality of an object consists entirely in its being an object of consciousness. Consequently, the greater the purity with which an object displays this character, the more truly real does it become. Now, the object of an illusory belief is distinguished from other so-called realities precisely by this fact, that it exists purely and simply for consciousness. Hence it, and it alone, attains *full* reality. An object is real precisely to the extent to which it is illusory. And it is to be observed that an illusion, as such, is pre-eminently and indisputably the work of the mind. It is thus proved, beyond cavil, that the real, in the only true sense of the word, is the work of the mind. The work of the mind is real, and the real is the work of the mind. In this way we escape from the fatal antithesis set up by the late Mr. Locke; to revert to which, as I have often shown, necessarily lands philosophy in a dead-Locke. I have, in fact, shown this so often, that this time I will leave Locke in his grave,[1] and will not even ex-Hume his great, but contemptible, successor.

The consciousness, however, which constitutes reality, though, of course, identical with our consciousness, cannot *be* our consciousness. I mean that it is our *consciousness* indeed, but it is not strictly *ours:* we have, so to speak, only a life interest in it. Objects do not begin to exist only when they begin to exist for *us.* It would, indeed, be distinctly inconvenient if we had to defer our birth until we knew all about our ancestors. In other words, it is clearly impossible to identify thought and reality if we take into account the fact that thought has a historical development. Which irrefragably proves that the fact alluded to must *not* be taken into account.[2] Hence the consciousness, which, by its relating activity, constitutes reality, is an *eternal* consciousness.

And the reality which is constituted by this eternal consciousness must be likewise timeless. For are not the reality and the consciousness one and the same? That both reality and the consciousness thereof must be timeless does indeed become obvious when we reflect that, as I am never weary of repeating, there is an absolute difference between succession and consciousness of succession. For this is to say that *if* succession were ever an object of consciousness, it would be absolutely different from the consciousness thereof—there would here be an absolute distinction between consciousness and its object. Which I have abundantly shown to be absurd. Hence succession is not so much as a possible object of thought.[3] To the eternal consciousness the long succession of events is as a tale that is told to the marines.

It now only remains to solve the apparent paradox that although consciousness is not, and cannot be, in time, it yet, with the characteristically inconceivable brutality of mere matter of fact, does have a development in time. The solution of the difficulty, if difficulty there be, is to be found in the fact that the expression "our consciousness" has the

[1] [*Thanks.*—ED., MIND!]

[2] Except, of course, so far as it enables us to argue that the judgment is real in *virtue* of having causes and effects.

[3] I was previously disposed to argue that successive events could only exist through the synthetic activity of thought; and that, as the object of thought, they were not successive. I argued, that is to say, that successive events, in virtue of involving the relation of succession, were not successive. But the view above given is, I think the intelligent reader will admit, more in harmony with the galling restrictions of logic.

misfortune to be afflicted with a peculiarly distressing form of ambiguity, whereby that expression stands indifferently for two things, which, though essentially identical, are so radically opposed one to the other as not to admit of being comprehended in a single conception. To explain : the conviction will assuredly have already forced itself upon the reader, not so much as a result of explicit reasoning to that effect as by the mere natural evolution of the argument as a whole, that the Eternal Consciousness has for content a divinely glorious and everlasting muddle ; and that it is, in truth, nothing less than what is described in the language of the (public) schools as 'the Eternal Cussedness of things'. Now 'our consciousness' may mean either of two things: either a function of our animal organism, which is being made, gradually and with occasional lapses into sense, a vehicle of the Eternal Cussedness ; or that Eternal Cussedness itself, as making the animal organism its vehicle, and subject to certain limitations in so doing, but retaining its essential characteristic of being in itself absolutely different from what it itself is, in so far as it is in time.

And, finally, this proof of the identity of thought and thing shows us the moral law as the very heart of reality. For while the mere question of fact may be regarded as conclusively settled by our argument, only in the light of ethical principle does its true significance stand fully revealed. In other words, what it all really *means* Goodness only knows.

V.—A TRIAD OF THE ABSOLUTE.

By H. Dele.

I.

Ὦ ὄν.

A contribution to the forthcoming *Hegelian Hymnal.*
(Republished by permission.)[1]

O Being for Self,
  O End of all Ends,
O Something, O Nothing
  Where everything blends!
Identical Absolute,
  Thee we acclaim,
Though empty of Content
  Thy vacuous Name.

True Sun of the Realm,
  Where the Bodiless move,
Insensible Object
  Of Sensuous Love,
Sole Pattern supernal,
  First Form without Stuff,
Why wasn't pure Being
  Existence enough?

Ah! why did you suffer
  The "slim" Demiurge
In endless Becoming
  Your Being to merge.
Oh! Where was your *Νοῦς*?
  Oh! What was the Good?
You resemble the Babes
  Who were lost in the Wood.[2]

[1] From the *Oxford Magazine*.

[2] *ὕλη*.

Oh ! why did you take
All the trouble and bother
Involved in becoming
A Manifold Other ?
Ah ! now you are Many,
You find it such Fun,
You'll never go back
To the Form of the One.

II.

A BALLADE OF YE ABSOLUTE.[1]

For the usage of a Hegelian Nursery.

The Absolute was very High—
More high than seasoned game ;
"I have been *kept* too long," It said,
"Identically Same".

The Absolute was very Broad—
It filled all Time and Space ;
It couldn't see Its Aspects—for
It hadn't got a face.

The Absolute lay very Low,
Veiled in a misty phrase ;
It was the only way, C——d said,
To elongate Its days.

The Absolute lay very Deep
In protoplastic Sludge,
With metaphysic fumes replete
And philosophic Fudge.

In Self-identity Alone,
Sans Father, Wife, or Mother,
It sobbed, "It would console me to
Be Something or An Other".

By Hegel's help It Was, and yet,
Its sad plight scarcely mended,
The fickle Elf returned to Self
Before Its hour was ended.

[1] Republished from the *Oxford Magazine.*

The Absolute for once to be
Intelligible sighed;
It read Itself in B——y's book,
And then, poor soul, It died.

III.

THE COMPLAINT OF THE ABSOLUTE.[1]

Remote, unfriended, melancholy, slow,
More slow than words can say,
I *Was*, unmixed, unfeeling, without go,
A Hamlet minus play.

Incarnate Boredom, absolute Ennui,
Oyster shut tight in shell,
Devil-less, defecated deity,
Heaven unenhanced by Hell.

And then—it almost makes me disbelieve
My own Totality:—
Through my 'unlimited inwards' passed a Heave
Of Spontaneity.

I felt a kind of Fidgets in my frame,
A twinge of Cosmic Schism;
I felt a little Other than the Same,
A nascent Dualism.

Was it a humid Vortex-ring that stirred,
Or dim primordial Cell?
The mirror of my consciousness was blurred,
I—wasn't very well.

Then—I forget the manner of the birth
Distraught by this world's worries:
But there proceeded from me with fell mirth
A scheme of Categories.

They took and bound me in a causal Chain,
To cure my trend chaotic:
On Mother Hegel's Syrup fed, my brain
Feels still quite idiotic.

Then as an *Aspect* from me there exhaled
My own efficient Double,
Him Cause, Creator, Demiurge I hailed;
He saves me all the trouble.

[1] Cp. *Pelican Record*, vol. v., No. 6.

And They and He between them this world made
  Of semblances and shows;
And what the Deuce it means I am afraid
  That no sane person knows.

I'm Everything and Nothing, here's my pain!
  Supreme, yet on the Shelf!
When shall I be my own true I again,
  Sweetly regarding Self?

VI.—SPECIMENS OF THE *CRITIQUE OF PURE ROT.*

By I. Cant.

From the Remains of a Philosopher.[1]

[*Note:* I must make time to translate the whole of this eye-opening work, being deeply sensible that to publish such bare outlines as these would do no justice to the author, especially in the matter of style, which I have translated as mere English, sacrificing the profundity of the original sentences that "have been measured by a carpenter," and whose dragon-tailed involutions of many a winding bout both de- and im-press the reader: he rightly judging that the effort of exegesis measures the value of the meaning when discovered, and compensates its absence when undiscoverable—labour being its own exceeding great reward: and which style I do not despair of imitating with the help of a certain brownish drench that I wot of: *verb. sap.*—S.T.C.]

CRITIQUE OF PURE ROT.

Preface.

Every new world-moving Philosophy is generated by a new method. Now my method of seeing things as they really are is to stand upon my head; for the images of all things being inverted on the retina, a man may by this means, in a manner, correct the perversity of nature without trusting to psycho-physiological processes that have the double fault of being mechanical and empirical. If any one think this an obvious device, I remind him of Copernicus and the egg.

The method was, to be sure, suggested to me by a Scotch philosopher's account of how the English open the eyes of their children by making them "see London". For one brief moment, flashing over in a whirligig, they beheld the

[1] It is known that Samuel Taylor Coleridge left much MS. (chiefly in the margins of his friends' books) that is still unpublished. We take it that this fragment was written in 1801, although (like Aristotle's works) it contains 'anticipations' that might suggest a later date; and we congratulate the readers of Mind! upon obtaining in 1901 a synopsis of doctrines so well calculated to initiate and direct the New Philosophy of a New Age.—Ed.

world in its true posture. This hint broke my dogmatic slumber. It explained why London merchants over-reach the rest of the world; for in youth, under the name of City-Arabs, they turn cart-wheels on the pavement, and thus learn to see things in their true relations: no one can be Lord-Mayor till he has turned 5,000 cart-wheels. Also English aristocrats, brow-beating a demagogue, accuse him of "turning everything upside down": such is their antipathy to popular education. But all this is English empiricism; whereas we begin with a *petitio principii* and proceed upon universal and necessary assertions *a priori*.

Book I., Part I., Chapter I., Article I.

§ 1, etc. Now, to cut matters short, let us begin by inquiring into the possibility of Rot in general. That Rot exists you may take my word. And there are two kinds of it: Damp Rot and Dry Rot, besides certain Fungoid Growths: but how are such things possible in the best of possible worlds?

Damp Rot being nothing else than the corruption of woody fibre, the possibility of it manifestly depends upon the presence of C and H_2O, into which the Manifold is received and judiciously distributed.

H_2O, popularly called 'water,' is an intuition and not a concept; for all water is *in* water and not *under* water. Moreover, water is *a priori*, since without it there could be no Damp Rot; but painting in water-colours absolutely presupposes water.

Similarly C is an intuition; for to intuit a thing is to *see* it. And the *a priori* necessity of C is given, in a manner, in the bare possibility of Music in general.

Thus the only possible genesis of Damp Rot is demonstrated as a synthetic construction in a pure heterogeneity. Only splash in the Manifold and the thing is done.

Observe, finally, that whilst C and H_2O are real as a matter of fact, yet on reflexion they are unreal. You will see this by standing on your head, and there is no other way of seeing it.

Book II. Transcendental Dodges of Blunderstanding, Part I., Chapter II., Article II.

§ 3. Well then, the possibility of Dry Rot depends on the system of the pure Caterwaulings, which are functions of Papperception, or Milk-for-babes.

To find the pure Caterwaulings need give us no trouble, as we may conveniently take them from the newspapers, and list them as follows :—

Quantity.	Quality.	Relation.	Modality.
Bottle	Imperialism	Pædagogue and Pupil	Ignorance
Half-bottles	Pro-Boerism	Praise and Profits	Prejudice
Bottle-and-a-half	The Closure	Log-rolling	Superstition

§ 4. Now there is a certain difficulty in applying these Caterwaulings to phenomena, which is not felt in distributing the Manifold within the province of Damp Rot. For if, as a matter of Damp Rot, I perceive that *a publisher is a fraud*, 'publisher' and 'fraud' are homogeneous intuitions in the synthesis of H_2O. For H_2O, being a synthetic function of Reason, is amenable to reasonable analysis, and (as the future will know) whatever is convenient is reasonable. Hence, a publisher being no doubt H (or *homo*), $_2O$ is the symbol of his fraud, meaning that he owes *too* much; and such an apprehension of the facts is both easy and elegant.

But if, in the sphere of Dry Rot, I judge that *a criticism in* MIND! *is praise,* how can such heterogeneous elements be brought together? For the 'criticism' is a given fact, whereas 'Praise' is pure Caterwauling. Now all such difficulties are overcome by scheming and skirmishing with C, which is the natural intermediary between pure Caterwaulings and all phenomena.

§ 5. To apply the pure Caterwaulings to matter-of-fact needs Imagination. This can surprise nobody; for all Philosophies are works of Imagination, or sportive essays in the fine art of Reason. In this case we want Imagination badly, and we will call it no mere imitative but 'productive Imagination,' because that sounds better. The labourer sings at his work; and in the severe work of labelling matters of fact with suitable Caterwaulings it is the function of Imagination to represent the pure Caterwaulings by generalised tunes in the form of C—that is, by the rhythms of tunes, abstracting from their particular notes and all heterogeneous sensuosity—such as a professor may hum without being able to sing them. They are called Sing-songs, and their correspondence with the Caterwaulings is exhibited in the following table :—

Caterwauling.	*Sing-song.*
Bottle.	The Leather Bottel.
Half-bottles.	Drink to Me Only with Thine Eyes.
Bottle-and-a-half.	We Won't Go Home till Morning.
Imperialism.	Rule Britannia.
Pro-Boerism.	Down among the Dead Men.
The Closure.	Donnybrook Fair.
Pædagogue and Pupil.	Said the Old Obadiah to the Young Obadiah.
Praise and Profits.	See the Conquering Hero.
Log-rolling.	The same, hummed alternately forwards and backwards.
Ignorance.	Nobody Knows What I Know.
Prejudice.	Sally in Our Alley.
Superstition.	Home, Sweet Home!

If with such incentives you can't stick the labels, I can't; and without standing on your head you will hardly be convinced that they stick fast.

§ 6. However, the humming of these Sing-songs by way of illustration may always be relied upon to enliven a lecture and to fill the class-room of the dullest pedant. The Sing-song of Log-rolling will be most effective if the professor, instead of humming it forwards and backwards alternately, shall hum it forwards and get his *famulus* to hum it backwards at the same time. This will illustrate the struggle for existence and demonstrate the special applicability of the third Caterwauling of Relation to Biology and social affairs.

§ 7. But further difficulties in applying the Caterwaulings to the Manifold may arise from not knowing which should be applied to what; so that whilst universally necessary they are particularly contingent: but here again the Sing-songs ought to help us. As to the Caterwaulings of Quality for example—if hastily and erroneously you call a man as big as yourself a Pro-Boer to the tune of *Down Among the Dead Men*, and he closes with you to the tune of *Rule Britannia*, there is a dead-lock whilst both sing *Donnybrook Fair*. Or again, in the Caterwaulings of Quantity—if you think you have drunk only Half-a-bottle, when in fact you have finished a Bottle-and-a-half, there is an irresistible impulse to sing *We Won't go Home till Morning;* and the chances are that you will even be late for breakfast, passing most of the interval in strict seclusion, and arriving fresh from an interview with the functionary at Bow Street. I shall show hereafter that the blame for all such slips lies ultimately at the door of the *Unding-an-sich;* but it will not be of much use, as the *Unding's* oak is always sported.

If after these illustrations any one fails to see how the Sing-songs help us in inflicting the Caterwaulings upon matters of fact, I can only say that it is a mystery hidden in the depths of the soul.

Book II., Part I., Walpurgisnacht, Chapter I., Article II.

§ 1. The worst thing you can do, my young friend, is to try to apply your blunderstanding to Ideas: it was never designed for such use and is quite incompetent. For the new dialectic shows that *noumena,* far from being the only objects of real knowledge, are just the things that the mind can't know. I cant.

Nevertheless, you can't help experimenting with Ideas; and thereby are generated three Fungoid Growths.

Chapter II., First Fungus: the Common Mushroom.

§ 2. Träume eines Geistersehers. . . .

. . . .

§ 3. Now all this fine confused thinking results from mistaking the Bottle of Papperception for Spirit *per se.*

Chapter III., Second Fungus: the Antilogistic Toadstool.

§ 3. Donnybrook Fair *in vacuo,* by our special Reporter. . . .

. . . .

Therefore, A is both B and not-B. Q.E.D.

But if A is B, it is impossible to know anything; and if it is not-B, it is impossible to believe anything; so since it is both, *tant pis.*

§ 4. The ground, however, of these conclusions (equally odd and inevitable) is, that we take A for granted; whereas *per se* it is not granted, but only Hay; and to make hay of A, or A of hay, is a solecism.

Chapter IV., Third Fungus.

§ 1. Die scholastische Götterdämmerung fängt an. . . .

. . . .

[*Note:* Angels and ministers of grace! least said, soonest mended. Indeed, there may be some things in this book which my friend Leighton would hardly sanction: it deserves to be not only translated but edited. Judicious commentators, however, will not be wanting:—

Wenn die Könige baun, haben die Kärrner zu thun.[1]

—S.T.C.]

[1] A translation that has been proposed for this verse:—

One fool makes many—

is more spirited than literal, and sacrifices urbanity to emphasis.—Ed.

VII.—SOME NEW APHORISMS OF HERAKLEITOS.

TRANSLATED BY PROFESSOR HYDATI.

THE importance of these new fragments will be readily understood when it is stated that they comprise no less than 44 dicta, while the total number of fragments of Herakleitos previously known was only 130. They were discovered, of course in Egypt, by Drs. Grenfell and Hunt, amid the ruins of a Ptolemaic hydropathic establishment in the Fayûm, on a palimpsest papyrus on which the rules of the institution had subsequently been inscribed. The curious will not fail to remark the irony of Fate whereby a water-cure both extinguished and preserved so much of the philosophy of Fire.

As might be expected from this state of affairs, the text is frequently difficult, but the well-known scholarship of Prof. Hydati puts the substantial accuracy of the translation of these interesting fragments beyond all doubt. Their authenticity also cannot be disputed: as Prof. Burnet well says, "They have unquestionably the true Herakleitean ring".[1] On the whole they are calculated only to deepen the impression, and to confirm the interpretation, of his previously ascertained doctrines. At the same time there is an engaging and outspoken modernity about some of the maxims, which seems to indicate that much of the obscurity the ancients complained of in Herakleitos may in reality have been due to the *prophetic character* of his thought and his marvellous prescience of modern conditions.

A. Personal Characteristics and Criticism of Society.

1.

I had rather be right than a king.

2.

It is more difficult to bridle one's tongue than a lively donkey.

3.

I have sought myself—and caught a Tartar![2]

[1] *Early Greek Philosophy*, p. 138, note.
[2] Only the first half of this saying was known before.

4.

I asked for Truth, and they gave me—History!

5.

I sent my book to the Bodleian, but the Board of Faculty did not read it—and granted me a degree!

6.

Asses prefer the sweepings of the lecture rooms to my original researches.

7.

Dullards think deep the darkness *they* cannot see through.

8.

'What *I* can understand, I despise,' says Sophomoros. Yet he wonders if I write obscurely.

9.

The seriousness of folly needs to be scorched with the inextinguishable laughter of the gods.

10.

Only the witless will try to winnow the wit from the chaff.

11.

The * *-ians are worthy to be strung up man by man, for that they drove away the best man among them, godlike * *-os saying, 'Behold he is too clever for us'.[1]

12.

Since *I* gave him beans, Pythagoras has eaten no others.[2]

13.

The Sophists of the * *[3] teach badly; else had they not taught * *[3] to deride them.

[1] Unfortunately the names are almost obliterated. If the remark is the same as that quoted in *Ritter und Preller* (ed. 7), p. 24, § 22, b., the exiling of Hermodoros by the Ephesians must be referred to. But Herakleitos was quite the man to express similar opinions on other cases also.

[2] The famous Pythagorean prohibition of beans, formerly supposed to have a mystical significance, is now usually derived from a primitive *taboo*. This dictum, however, suggests a simpler explanation.

[3] Names illegible.

14.

Learning does not teach sense: else had it taught—many whom the libel laws forbid me to mention.[1]

15.

They who seek for gold turn a ton of rock into dust and get ten pennyweights.[2]

16.

The filleted soul is the best.[3]

17.

The mob must fight for its law as for its wall: but the weakest go to the wall.[4]

B. The Game of Life and its Paradoxes.

18.

The World is a Demon's play, and all must play a game that none may understand. But the wise play upon words.

19.

Of the gods man's understanding is misunderstanding.

20.

Life is a play, largely upon words.

21.

In waking we are asleep to our dreams to which we wake in sleeping. And yet men will not credit dreams of better worlds.[5]

22.

They send expeditions to all places but to Hades, which awaits them all and holds far more than they desire to know.[6]

23.

It is better to bury the body than the soul, and yet men dread the one and think nothing of the other.

[1] A more cautiously reticent version of a famous dictum.
[2] Cp. *R.P.*, p. 35, § 36 b.
[3] This allusion to the classical custom of adorning sacrificial victims with fillets seems to be a wonderful anticipation of the moral value of *self-sacrifice*.
[4] Cp. *R.P.*, p. 38, § 40. [5] Cp. *ibid.*, p. 36, § 38. [6] Cp. *ibid.*

24.

Souls smell in Hades—would that bodies did not reek on earth.[1]

25.

Dry souls are best—to burn.[2]

26.

The hidden jest is the best.[3]

C. The Flux, the Fire and the Union of Opposites.

27.

All things flow and nothing endures—except the rot that is poured forth in the Schools.

28.

None can pass the same examination twice, and many not even once.

29.

They are honoured and not honoured—they are gulphed.

30.

The war[4] is the father of all things, but its paternity also is a matter of opinion.

31.

One cannot love the same woman twice, nor most even once.

32.

Wisdom to all men is commons;[5] for by them is nourished high thinking.

33.

Three things are evil for thinking—rollers, chapels, and battells; for they dampen the ardour of students.

34.

Jesting and earnest are the same; for out of jesting comes earnest, and earnestness turns into jest.

[1] Cp. *R.P.*, p. 37, § 38 d.
[2] Completes and makes sense of a well-known saying.
[3] Cp. *R.P.*, § 27. [4] ὁ πόλεμος. [5] τὰ ξυνά, cp. *R.P.*, p. 35.

35.

'Tis the strain of the labouring bow that speedeth the arrow.

36.

Out of seriousness cometh forth mirth and into seriousness turneth again.

37.

Nay, but he who is wise will traverse the two ways together,
Mirthful in serious work, seriously aiming in mirth.[1]

38.

There is a way to lecture and a way not. But the drier way is better than the damper.

39.

There is a way to lecture and a way from lecture; and the way to and the way from are the same: it is a short cut.

40.

The Eagle both feeds on the Vitals of Prometheus and does not feed on his *Vitals*. For Prometheus does not die. So also is the World consumed by the Fire and not consumed.

41.

When highborn dames catch *Tunnies* with a bait of gold, then shall the Flux of Words be stayed, and what I *mean* be manifest to all.

42.

The new lives in the death of the true, the true in the death of the false, the false in the death of the new. Are not truth, then, and falsehood the same? And is not the new of two things one, either itself false, or what renders all else false?

43.

Wit is the Phœnix who burns himself and is rekindled from the ashes of his father.

44.

The way Up and the way Down is the same, namely the Great Western.

[1] These last aphorisms seem to be metrical, and indeed elegiacs. That Herakleitos should have written poetry will surprise no one who realises what difficulty he had to express himself in prose.

VIII.—PRE-SOCRATIC PHILOSOPHY.

By Lord Pilkington (of Milkington).

There was a time before the teaching of philosophy had taken the form of a dictation lesson, when students ventured beyond the covers of their note-book and even attempted a little dialectic on their own account. Small blame to them if their Dialogue sometimes assumed a playful air, or if, in those walks up Shotover or round the Hinkseys and the 'Happy Valley,' which have lost their charm for cycling Oxford of the present generation, they capped each other in amœbean verse like Vergil's shepherds. As a remembrance of these happier methods of study, which the publication of Mind! may do something to revive, we print, before they are forgotten, a few fragments upon the Pre-Socratics which originated under the conditions described.

Damon.

The Ionic philosophers trace
The World to a physical base:—
Thus while Thales sought a
First '*Αρχὴ* in Water
Anaximenes put Air in its place.

Pythias.

From the Concrete Xenophanes fleeing
Found the world to consist in pure Being;
Said, '*Πᾶν* = *Ἕν*,'
And 'Gods ain't like men,
But all-thinking and hearing and seeing'.[1]

Damon.

Heracleitus said everything came
From a Strife which he sometimes calls Flame.
The illustrious Hegel
Thought this quite '*en règle*,'
Meaning '*Seyn* and *Nicht-seyn* are the same'.

[1] See *Ritter und Preller*, p. 79, § 85.

Pythias.

It's all very well when you're tight
To say that white's black, and black white;
    But this never will do,
    As Parmenides knew,
For the Footpath which leads to the Right.[1]

Damon.

There was an old man of Abdera
Whose language grew queerer and queerer;
    With his ***Δὲν*** and his ***Κρᾶσις***
    And other odd phrases
He perplexed the good folk of Abdera.

Pythias.

Pythagoras thought that Creation
Was a mere Arithmetic Relation,
    Said 'you must not eat beans
    By no manner of means,'
And believed in the Soul's Transmigration.

[1] See *Ritter und Preller*, p. 88, § 94.

IX.—NEW PLATONIC DIALOGUES.

I.—AN APORIA.[1]

JONES was a congenital genius, and we always expected he would come to a bad end, poor fellow. Hence I was not surprised to find that after an early marriage and a brief but brilliant matrimonial career (including two pairs of twins and a triplet), he should have taken up his residence in an asylum which shall be nameless, but where I occasionally visit him. The doctors consider him a hopeless case, but the chief thing I can find the matter with him is an excessive conscientiousness which unfits him for practical work and leads him to raise scruples about what everybody else takes for granted. For instance, the last time I saw him he startled me with a fallacy which seemed to me not unworthy of mention by the side of the *Liar* and the *Crocodile*.

Jones had been greatly depressed; he declared himself a murderer, and would not be comforted. Suddenly he asked me a question. 'Are not the parents the cause of the birth of their children?' said he. 'I suppose so,' said I. 'Are not all men mortal?' 'That also may be admitted.' 'Then are not the parents the cause of the death of their children, since they know that they are mortal? And am I not a murderer?' I was, I own, puzzled. At last I thought of something soothing. I pointed out to Jones that to cause the death of another was not necessarily murder. It might be manslaughter or justifiable homicide. 'Of which of these then am I guilty?" he queried. I could not say because I had never seen the Jones family, but I hear Jones has become a great bore in the asylum by his unceasing appeals to every one to tell him whether he has committed murder, manslaughter, or justifiable homicide!

Curiously enough, when I told the tale to a learned friend of mine, he showed me what appears to be a new fragment of Plato's *Lysis*, on an Egyptian papyrus recently discovered. It distinctly anticipates Jones in its statement of the prob-

[1] Cp. *Pelican Record*, vol. iv., No. 4.

lem, and testifies aloud to the saying that there is nothing new under the sun, and that truth is eternal.

ΣΚΩΠΤΑΔΗΣ,[1] *ΛΥΣΙΣ.*

S. Whom then, Lysis, do you consider your best friends, and love most? *L.* My father and my mother, as is most fitting. *S.* Why do you so love them? *L.* Both for other reasons and because they are the cause of my living. *S.* And does that seem to you a great benefit? *L.* Surely the greatest of all. *S.* What then do you esteem the greatest evil? *L.* Of all evils death seems to me the greatest and most hateful. *S.* Then you would not love those who are the cause of your coming death (*τοῦ μέλλοντος θανάτου*), if you knew them? *L.* That is impossible. *S.* And what would you call those who knowingly cause the death of others? *L.* Evil-doers and murderers. *S.* You would not call them your friends? *L.* Certainly not; for did you not convince me that a friend does good only to his friend, and not evil. *S.* And yet perhaps, Lysis, you escape your own notice loving your own murderers, and thinking them your greatest friends. *L.* I do not understand you, Skoptades. *S.* Tell me, Lysis, are not all men mortal? *L.* Assuredly. *S.* Then all who are born must also die? *L.* Of course. *S.* And if any one knowingly put you in a place where you must die, such as a desert island or a den of lions, would you not consider him the cause of your death? *L.* Most certainly I should. *S.* But have not your parents done this very thing to you? *L.* How so? *S.* Did you not say that they were the authors of your being in a world where you must die? *L.* So it would appear. *S.* And does it not follow that they are the authors of the greatest evil, namely death, and not friends, but murderers? *L.* By Zeus, Skoptades, the argument has turned out a most unholy one. *S.* And the worst of it is that we do not yet know what is a friend and whom we ought to love most. . . .

This then is the *ἀπορία* of the *Lysis;* but what is the *λύσις* of the *ἀπορία*?

II.—A Sequel to the *Republic.*[2]

The following interesting fragment of a Platonic dialogue has been found on a papyrus recently discovered in the belly of an ancient crocodile of literary tastes, which Messrs.

[1] This is the MS. reading, but ΣΩΚΡΑΤΗΣ surely must be intended.
[2] Cp. *Pelican Record*, vol. v., No. 5.

Grenfell and Hunt have imported from Egypt. With their leave we publish a translation, which will doubtless be recognised as the most important addition to our knowledge of Plato's lost writings since the recovery of the fragment of the *Lysis* printed above.

ΣΩΚΡΑΤΗΣ, ΚΕΦΑΛΟΣ, ΠΛΑΤΩΝ.

Soc. Methinks, Plato, I see Kephalos hastening round the corner into yonder side-street. Will you not quickly run after him and tell him that it is not good for a man at his age to be in such haste, and that moreover we have seen him, and that he cannot escape us, since there is no thoroughfare at the other end?

Plato. Assuredly, Socrates, I will put on my running foot.

Soc. I hail thee, Kephalos, breathless though I am. It seems to me a long time since I met you. Indeed I do not think I have seen you since we visited you at your house on the festival of Bendis and had a famous argument on the nature of Justice.

Keph. I think you are right.

S. It was a great pity you did not stay and listen to the whole argument.

K. I had to go out and attend to some domestic matters.

S. You *said* it was a sacrifice.

K. You are right again, Socrates, as I now remember.

S. It must have been a very long sacrifice.

K. The argument, too, was very long, I have heard.

S. Nevertheless, you would have enjoyed it. But it does not matter; Plato here has written it all out beautifully and he shall send you a copy. You deserve it in return for the drinks wherewith we kept up our spirits in the long search for justice.[1]

K. I thank you both.

S. And now, Kephalos, while we accompany you home to the Piræus, I want to ask you concerning a point which I was eager to inquire into when last we met, but which escaped my notice owing to your[2] having raised the question of justice. It is this. You are rich, are you not?

K. Moderately so.

S. To whom then do you intend to leave your riches when you die?

K. To my children, of course.

[1] There is no mention of them in the existing MSS. of the *Republic*.

[2] Our traditional account hardly bears this out.

3

S. I thought you would say this. But tell me why you propose to do this?

K. Because they stand first in my love, I suppose.

S. Ah! I am afraid, Kephalos, that is impossible.

K. Are you not escaping your own notice talking nonsense?

S. I wish I were. But it really is impossible and contrary to nature for you to love your own children first.

K. How so?

S. You must first love other people's children and then your own.

K. I do not understand you.

S. How can you, being a man, have children of your own to love until you have first loved the children of others?[1]

K. By Zeus, Socrates, you are right. For he alone of the gods could do what you say, if indeed he was the only parent of Athena.

S. You agree then that it is absurd to love your own children first, and on this account to leave the money to them rather than to those of others?

K. I suppose so.

S. Consider this also. Do you not wish good to your children?

K. Of course.

S. Then you do not wish that they should get that which would harm them?

K. Certainly not.

S. But are not good things bad for the bad?

K. Very likely.

S. Then wealth being a good thing in itself will be bad for the bad?

K. This we see in many cases.

S. In proportion then as your children are bad it will harm them to have wealth?

K. So at least the argument shows.

S. You ought not therefore to leave your wealth to them.

K. Would you have me leave it to my enemies?

S. Not at all.

K. To whom then?

S. To those to whom the intrinsically good is really good.

K. Are you thinking of yourself, Socrates?

S. Have you never heard of my Little Demon (*δαιμόνιον*)?

[1] An indignant scholiast—probably an Alexandrine—has here written in the margin, 'Look at the Greek, Socrates; look at the Greek'. But Socrates was no doubt quite capable of using *φιλεῖν* in the sense of *ἐρᾶν*.

And would not the wealth which benefited me do harm to Xanthippe?

K. I doubt whether she would get much of it.

S. Even if I took care to prevent this, would it not make her temper worse to think of me spending my wealth in the the pursuit of the beautiful?

K. Your pursuit would always be in vain.

S. That is why I am a philosopher. Still, as you know, we Athenians φιλοκαλοῦμεν μετ' εὐτελείας.[1]

K. So I have observed. But will you not finish telling me to whom I ought to leave my wealth?

S. Most willingly. Do you know Plato here?

K. Yes, and I have long desired to ask him whether he be truly the son of Apollon as well as the descendant of Poseidon. He certainly looks it.

S. Hush! you see how he blushes. Plato, let me tell you, is about to found an Academy, the first there has been, and the most famous there ever will be. How better could you bestow your wealth than by giving it to Plato's Academy?

K. I would rather leave it to Xanthippe!

S. Even if we promise you immortality of fame?

K. You are far more likely to confer an eternity of infamy. However, I will do what you ask on one condition, and that is that you, Plato, should write down this conversation exactly as it occurred, in order that men may know whether Socrates always got the better in words of those he conversed with.

P. I agree, Kephalos.

S. And I no less; I will this time content myself with getting the better in deeds, if only they be good.

III.—Congratulations.[2]

ΣΩΚΡΑΤΗΣ, ΧΑΡΜΙΔΗΣ.

Socrates. What ho! Charmides, whither away?

Charmides. Excuse my haste, Socrates, if I cannot stay to converse with you.

S. Why, what is the matter?

C. Have you not heard that Milanion is to be married to-morrow, and that he has asked me to help him prepare for the occasion?

S. Every word of this is news indeed.

[1] Love the beautiful on the cheap.
[2] Cp. *Pelican Record,* vol. v., No. 6.

C. Well, then, come with me now and congratulate him.

S. Come with you I will and with pleasure, going third myself. But whether I should congratulate Milanion deserves further inquiry.

C. Why, he is the happiest of mortals, and not even you could argue him out of this belief!

S. Or *thinks* he is. But tell me why; who is the cause?

C. He has a good one. He is going to marry Atalanta.

S. What, Atalanta, the daughter of Atlas! (*Whistles.*) You astonish me.

C. Yes, it surprised us all. Not of course that *he* should be in love with her—they all were that. But even now I can hardly understand why she took him. For does it not seem strange that the fairest, noblest, richest, and cleverest girl in Greece should choose Milanion, who, though an honest fellow enough and a great friend of mine, is only very moderately endowed in all these respects?

S. Is she not also the fastest girl in Greece?

C. Oh, yes, fast enough to catch or to get away from us all. But that makes it all the absurder that she should actually marry a Milanion after rejecting all the best men by the dozen!

S. Yes, I have heard that was her custom. But tell me, were *you* also among her victims?

C. No, Socrates; how can you think that? I could never have put up with a girl that gave herself such airs. Still I confess I was a little piqued that she would never take any notice of me, who am, as you know, generally considered to be somewhat fascinating myself.

S. I should be the last person in the world to deny *that.* But you and Atalanta would clearly never have got on together. You are both too megalopsychic, and you know that two of a trade never agree.

C. Still she might have chosen some one less commonplace than Milanion. He is frightfully in love with her of course, and by nature kind and obliging and capable of any amount of devotion, but somehow it does not seem fitting that so glorious a girl should throw herself away like that. Can you understand it?

S. Perhaps you have escaped your own notice answering your own question.

C. How so?

S. Did you not say that he loved her exceedingly? Perhaps she loves to be loved.

C. You may be right. Certainly, you never saw anything so absurd. He calls her his only goddess, and positively worships her.

S. What you now say, Charmides, makes me certain that I must not go on and congratulate Milanion.

C. Why not, Socrates?

S. The poor fellow can never be happy.

C. Not even with a visible goddess of his own selection, whom he can be with always?

S. Just because of the advantages you mention.

C. I do not understand.

S. Do you believe in the gods, Charmides?

C. Of course I do, like every one else.

S. Then you worship them?

C. Certainly, whenever it is convenient.

S. And do you spend a long time every day in worshipping them?

C. Not perhaps a very great part of the day. Still I never pass an image of Zeus or Athene or Aphrodite without showing them the proper respect.

S. You would not, however, think of worshipping the gods all day long?

C. Well, perhaps that would be a little tiresome.

S. Nor would you wish to worship at the same shrine always?

C. No; I thank the gods often that they are many.

S. And yet, Charmides, you thought Milanion would be happy because he could be with his goddess always and worship the same for ever.

C. I had not thought of what you now persuade me.

S. It seems then that it is not good to worship always, and that I must not congratulate Milanion.

C. So it would seem.

S. And we must consider this also, whether it is good to be worshipped, and whether I may congratulate Atalanta.

C. At all events you should go there and try, Socrates. It is worth going a long way to see Atalanta, especially if one has not yet seen her. And if one has, it seems still better worth going. She, moreover, will be glad to see you. I have often heard her say that she thought you must be the funniest old thing in Athens, and that she wished you would not confine your conversations to young men and, well, women like Diotima the Mantinean.[1]

S. You see how even my virtue may be misconstrued!

[1] Cp. *Symposium*, 201 D.

Nevertheless I will go, if I can make sure that she deserves my congratulations. But I greatly fear she does not.

C. Why?

S. To be worshipped always is perhaps still more difficult than to worship always, especially for one human and, in addition, a woman.

C. That seems a hard saying, and I hope you will explain it.

S. Willingly. Would you not allow that all things in the world have their proper excellence, and only then deserve to be called good when they act in accordance with it?

C. Certainly, seeing that I cannot hinder it.

S. Then I suppose a god also must have his proper virtue or excellence?

C. Perhaps.

S. What then would you say it was?

C. To be as divine as possible.

S. And what would you say was the proper excellence of man?

C. To be human and to think human things.

S. Very good. Then is it part of the divine excellence to walk about and go to market like a man?

C. That would be ridiculous. A god must stay unruffled on his pedestal and look dignified.

S. And if a man behaved similarly, what would you think?

C. I should think it very unseemly.

S. And do you not think that he would also find it very uncomfortable to be always raised aloft on a pedestal in all weathers, and to live so splendid and holy a life?

C. By Zeus he would, especially when the young men came to paint him red.

S. And do you think a girl would find this more agreeable?

C. She might at first, but, I fancy, would soon grow weary.

S. Aye, and run away with the first man that was strong enough to lift her off her pedestal, even though he was a brutal athlete or an irreverent fellow of the baser sort.

C. I think you are very likely right.

S. Was it not then a reasonable girl who answered Nausiknides the Philosopher, desiring to marry her, that she could not live so high up in the air, nor was she fit to consort with a god?

C. I suppose she saved herself and him much misery.

S. It seems then that it is contrary to her proper nature for Atalanta to be treated as a goddess, and that, if he does this, Milanion will only make her miserable, whichever happens, while not becoming happy himself.

C. By Athene, that is the most sensible and consoling

thing that has yet been said about this unhappy affair! Of course you must *not* congratulate Atalanta. We must try to save her. I will go therefore and tell her what you say. I am sure she will be grateful to you for saving her from so terrible a fate. And the next time you meet her, I should not wonder if she kissed you.

S. I think, Charmides, you are too hasty and not yet accustomed to regard these matters philosophically. At any rate do not forget to tell Atalanta that you love her far more than Milanion ever could. As for me, I should prefer not to be kissed by her nor to be mentioned by you; indeed, I would almost rather meet Xanthippe than Atalanta, after you have told her all this—if she really loves Milanion.

X.—THE LADIES' ARISTOTLE.

I.—The Great-souled Woman.

This interesting new fragment of Aristotle has recently been published in the *Proceedings of the Society for Megalopsychical Research*, and we have obtained permission to republish it for the benefit of the readers of Mind![1] Internal evidence leaves no doubt of its authenticity, and though in the present unenlightened state of public opinion it is hardly possible to divulge the methods whereby it was obtained, it may confidently be predicted that all students of Aristotle will at once recognise what a gap it fills in the *Ethics* of that great thinker, and how completely it disposes of the notion that his work was intended for men only.

'Concerning the megalopsychic man, then, let so much have been said. But it follows to speak concerning the megalopsychic *woman*, not indeed worthily, but as a mere man may. For as we said before, it is the part of the 'Varsity man (τοῦ πεπαιδευμένου[2]) to demand only such exactness (ἐπὶ τοσοῦτον τἀκριβὲς ἐπιζητεῖν) as is compatible with the subject, but of the megalopsychic woman 10,000 mathematicians would demand exactness in vain.

'She produces indeed no slight aporia in other respects also, first of all, whether she exist or not. But *we* say that the actuality (ἐνέργειαν) is prior to the potentiality (δυνάμεως); it is absurd therefore that the fairest form (κάλλιστον εἶδος) of female virtue should not exist in actuality in a cosmos wherein all things are as lovely as they can be.[3]

'Likewise it is objected to her that in the matter of virtue she is unlike the other so-called virtuous women, but wittingly or unwittingly such people say nought (οὐδὲν λέγουσι). For it has been laid down that great-souledness is greatness in all the virtues, and this the megalopsychic woman possesses. For she does all things for the sake of the Beautiful (διὰ τὸ καλόν), and only those possessing complete virtue do this.

[1] Cp. also *The Pelican Record*, vol. v., No. 2, p. 45.
[2] Cp. *Eth. Nic.*, i., 3, 4. [3] Cp. *ibid.*, i., 9, 5.

'It is necessary therefore that she should be not only supremely good, but also surpassingly beautiful.

'Now this is the reason why she is so rare; for it is by nature difficult to be beautiful, and still more to remain so throughout a perfect life.[1] And even by art it is not possible to be beautiful much beyond the limits of one's given material (ὕλη).

'But it is easy to see that from her beauty, being one, all the other excellences and goods follow of necessity. For her beauty is the whole of virtue viewed in relation to others (ἐν τῷ πρὸς ἕτερον[2]).

'Hence she will appear witty and wise and generous and temperate to all who behold her. And what appears to all, that we say is (ἃ γὰρ πᾶσι δοκεῖ ταῦτ' εἶναί φαμεν[3]).

'And further, all the external goods will be added to her. Whether indeed she should have a husband is disputed (if indeed a husband be a good of any sort), but it is evident that she can have as many as she desires, and that she will not lead a solitary life (βίον μονώτην). Nor will she lack honours, though no honour could possibly be worthy of her complete excellence.[4] And nobility and great wealth also will be hers, whether she acquire them with her husband or from those who seek to honour her.

'Thus she will be able to exhibit the virtue of Magnificence also, though her entertainments will be few and great and much talked about, rather than many and petty. Nevertheless she will frequent entertainments of all sorts, for she would prefer to enjoy intense pleasure for the season rather than a prolongation of the humdrum, and to live one year fashionably rather than many obscurely.[5]

'Nevertheless she will think lightly of them, nor will she talk to women; wherefore she will seem to look down upon all.[6]

'In matters of dress however her taste will be perfect, and avoiding the extremes both of excess and defect, she will wear neither too much nor too little, but the right amount to display her beauty, in accordance with the due proportion (κατὰ τὸν ὀρθὸν λόγον). And on this account also she must be beautiful, for without beauty it is not easy to bear gracefully the "happy creations" of the dressmaker (φέρειν ἐμμελῶς τὰ εὐτυχήματα[7]).

'Wherefore also she will be tall and with a good figure

[1] Cp. *Eth. Nic.*, i., 7, 16.
[2] Cp. *ibid.*, v., 1, 20.
[3] Cp. *ibid.*, x., 2, 4.
[4] Cp. *ibid.*, iv., 3, 17.
[5] Cp. *ibid.*, ix., 8, 9.
[6] Cp. *ibid.*, iv., 3, 18.
[7] Cp. *ibid.*, iv., 3, 21.

(for beauty implies stature, and tiny women may be neat and symmetrical but not beautiful[1]). And indeed that her body should be great is necessary also on account of the greatness of her soul. For the soul is intended by nature to rule the body, and it would be unworthy of a great soul to rule a small body.

'And moreover her walk will be slow and stately, and her voice measured and thrilling[2]; it would not befit her to lift up her skirts and run,[3] except for the sake of something glorious and beautiful, like Atalanta.

'But whether she will be in love, it is not easy to say. For on the one hand love seems to be of the goods, but on the other, whom should she love? For love is the part of the inferior who cannot sufficiently honour his superior,[4] but the megalopsychic woman has no superior. But if some say that she should love the megalopsychic man, we reply that no one could possibly do *that*. Wherefore it is more fitting that she should receive the love and honour of all she looks upon, but without loving them in return. For why should she? That would be absurd (*ἄτοπον γάρ*).

'It remains therefore that the megalopsychic woman is a lover, not of others, but of herself, because of the Beautiful. And, as has been said,[5] Self-love is good, and being good, the megalopsychic woman must love herself (*δεῖ φίλαυτον εἶναι*). But not like the many (*ὡς δ' οἱ πολλοί οὐ χρή*), for *they* are not beautiful. And thus she will plainly be self-sufficing, and also beautiful, and yet have many friends to display the happiness of her life (*εἰς ἐπίδειξιν τῆς εὐδαιμονίας*).

'Nevertheless she will sacrifice them all, and her husband and her children, and her wealth and her health, for the sake of the Beautiful. Aye, and if need be, she will even die for the sake of it, choosing it in preference to all else, and attributing a greater share of it to herself than to others.[6] If indeed she should become involved in the old age and misfortunes of a Hecuba,[7] and should not escape her own notice losing her beauty, her happiness would be impaired and she would become miserable (*ἀθλία*): but this is not probable (*ἀλλ' οὐκ εἰκός*).'

PS. At the last moment we find, from a note for which we are indebted to Prof. Stewart's unsurpassed Aristotelian learning, that a totally different view is taken in the *Magna*

[1] Cp. *Eth. Nic.*, iv., 3, 5.
[2] Cp. *ibid.*, iv., 3, 35.
[3] Cp. *ibid.*, iv., 3, 15.
[4] Cp. *ibid.*, viii, 8, 4-5.
[5] Cp. *ibid.*, ix., 8, 11.
[6] Cp. *ibid.*, ix., 8, 9.
[7] Cp. *ibid.*, i., 10, 14.

Moralia of the megalopsychic woman, which shows that the later Aristotelians were incapable of sustaining the lofty ideal of feminine perfection which their master had put before them. The curious may look for the original of the appended translation on page 540 of the first volume of Prof. Stewart's *Notes on the Nicomachean Ethics* :—

'Enough has now been said about the Great-souled man.

'The Great-souled woman remains, and causes difficulty: for the question has been raised whether Woman has a soul. The *Girl-Undergrad* of Euripides indeed says, "In Hockey is my soul," thus declaring plainly that the soul is not an essential principle within her, but an accident without. Perhaps however it would be too unkind and heterodox to maintain absolutely that Woman has no soul; but how, on the other hand, can she be Great-souled, if Greatness of soul is the ornament of its possessor and causes him to speak with a deep voice, whereas

'"Silence is the ornament of Woman"?

'Moreover, Man conquered at Olympia,[1] but Woman never, which makes a great difference; and if a great difference, then a difference in respect of that which is essential—the soul. Therefore, since Man is Great-souled, it follows that Woman is not Great-souled.

'So much for the conclusion which follows logically.

'We might also consider the subject physically, taking account of the Nature of Things: but the inquiry would be very tedious; for, as Homer says in the *Margites*,

'"The world is full of a number of things".

'We have said enough, however, to show that the Woman mentioned above is an Impossible Woman.'

Ed., Mind!

II.—The Brave Woman.[2]

It is with no slight gratification that we continue the publication of the better half of the *Ethics*, *viz.*, that devoted to showing how the acerbities of masculine virtue must be modified and mitigated to fit the delicacies of feminine idiosyncrasy. The 'brave woman' is not, indeed, cast in so heroic a mould as the megalopsychic paragon of feminine excellence, nor does Aristotle so obviously surpass the limits of scientific sobriety in describing her; but no one can read his account without feeling that Aristotle is here exhibiting

[1] Cp. *Eth. Nic.*, vii., 4, 2. [2] Cp. *Pelican Record*, vol. v., No. 4.

in its full profundity that subtle comprehension of feminine character which he derived from his life-long observation and varied matrimonial experience. Plato, assuredly, could never have written thus, and even the wisdom of Solomon pales in comparison!

'The brave man then, as has been said, preserves the Mean between rashness and cowardice with respect to the grounds of fear and confidence, attaining the Beautiful in war, not without pleasure if he be successful, even though not without painful exertion. Whence a difficulty arises whether *women* also are to be considered brave, and if so, how.[1]

'For some indeed maintaining an absurd thesis contend that, rightly trained, women are in no wise less brave than men, being inferior in strength alone,[2] and as illustrations adduce Amazons and Spartan women and if any elsewhere among other barbarians take part in war. Wherefore also the investigation has become very invidious, owing to friends of ours introducing lady guardians,[3] who desire eagerly to share in political rights. Nevertheless it would seem better, and even necessary, in order to save the constitution, to upset even one's own household (*καίτοι δόξειεν ἂν δεῖν ἐπὶ σωτηρίᾳ γε τῆς πολιτείας καὶ τὴν οἰκείαν οἰκίαν ἀναιρεῖν*), and even though we be philosophers to prefer truth to politeness, even where women are in question, maintaining stoutly that their courage is other than that of men.[4]

'It is needful therefore to reject such paradoxes, leaving alone the legendary Amazons and remembering how the boasted Spartan women behaved[5] during the Theban invasion; while as for the barbarians, it does not befit a cultivated man to expect exactness in all the plausible tales which are told about them.[6]

'But the nature of feminine bravery will become clear if we inquire more physically what is most terrible to them, and wherein the beauty of their bravery shines out most.

'For just as the Good is not one and the same for all, but different things are good and terrible by nature for men and for fishes—for fishes indeed water is good and air bad, but

[1] Ὅθεν ἀπορεῖται εἰ καὶ τὰς γυναῖκας ἀνδρείας νομιστέον, καὶ πῶς.

[2] A plain but polemical reference to Plato, *Rep.*, 452 foll.

[3] Διὸ καὶ λίαν προσάντης γεγένηται ἡ ζήτησις διὰ τὸ φίλους ἄνδρας εἰσαγαγεῖν τὰς φύλακας, σφόδρα βουλομένας μετέχειν τοῦ ἄρχειν καὶ ἄρχεσθαι.

[4] Τὴν ἀνδρείαν ἑτέραν εἶναι τοῦ ἀνδρείου. Cp. *Eth. Nic.*, i., 6, 1.

[5] Τὰς μὲν μεμυθολογημένας Ἀμαζόνας ἐῶντας χαίρειν. Cp. *Politics*, ii., 9, 1270, b. 33.

[6] Ἐν τοῖς πιθανολογουμένοις περὶ αὐτῶν. Cp. *Eth. Nic.*, i., 3, 4.

for men, contrariwise,[1] so, too, the terrible is not the same for men and for women, and the habit of the brave woman is so called by analogy. For their work is different, and virtue is relative to work.[2]

'Neither do those say well who maintain that the bravery of women is relative to their amusement (*παιδία*), instancing such as fearlessly carry many talents' worth of jewels into a crowded theatre. For the Good is earnest[3] and as Hesiod says:—

'"Life is real, life is earnest".

It is manifest, therefore, that the Good not even of woman is attained in amusement, but in work. Now in man's case his work is admittedly to live well and act well as a citizen, but about woman they dispute, though a work she must have, if she be not by nature devoid of a share in human excellence.[4] Now the many say it is to look well and dress well, with whom also Homer agrees, declaring that

'"Variegated dresses are the work of women,"[5]

and

'"Dresses, thin, of fine fabric which are the work of women".[6]

But men of the world and of repute say rather it is housekeeping and the bearing of lawful children. Or, should we add, the capacity to call and to be called on?[7]

'About what things then concerned with their work are women brave? About death in housekeeping? But this is absurd, for of this no one dies, except by accident. Or in childbirth? But this all fear, being human, unless indeed one should be mad or without sensibility, as they say some of the barbarians are.[8] Nor indeed is there anything beautiful in such a death.

'It remains, therefore, that the fear in regard to which a woman is called brave should be loss of reputation (*ἀδοξία*).[9] For this is most terrible to every sensible woman. But the brave woman nevertheless will run the risk of this, doing 10,000 things contrary to custom, for the sake of the Beauti-

[1] *Καθάπερ γὰρ τἀγαθὸν οὐχ ἕν, οὐδὲ ταὐτὸ πᾶσιν, ἀλλὰ ἕτερα ἀγαθὰ καὶ φοβερὰ φύσει ἀνθρώποις καὶ ἰχθύσι—τοῖς μὲν γὰρ ὕδωρ ἀγαθὸν καὶ ἀὴρ κακόν, τοῖς δ' ἐναντίως.* Cp. *Eth. Nic.*, vi., 7, 4.

[2] *Τὸ γὰρ ἔργον ἕτερον, ἡ δ' ἀρετὴ πρὸς τὸ ἔργον.*

[3] *Τὸ γὰρ ἀγαθὸν σπουδαῖον.*

[4] *Εἴπερ μὴ τῆς ἀνθρωπικῆς ἀρετῆς ἄμοιρος πέφυκε.* Cp. *Eth. Nic.*, i., 13, 14.

[5] *Πέπλοι παμποίκιλοι ἔργα γυναικῶν.* *Iliad*, vi., 289.

[6] *Od.*, vii., 96.

[7] *Ἢ προσθετέον τὸ δύνασθαι καλεῖν καὶ καλεῖσθαι;*

[8] Cp. *Eth. Nic.*, iii., 7, 7.

[9] Cp., *ibid.*, iii., 7, 1.

ful. Not but what she will fear such things, but she will fear them as she should, and when, and where, and as is reasonable: and she who will endure them for the sake of the Beautiful is truly brave and intrepid for a woman.[1]

'Whereas she who exceeds in fearlessness hardly exists, even though there are some who do not fear even a divorce, as they say of certain of the Hyperatlanteans.[2] And she is nameless—for indeed it will not do to mention names—being also very rare; yet might one call her a "bold bad" woman.[3]

'For the most part, however, women incline rather to the opposite extreme of excessive fear of the customary, and follow all the fashions slavishly; for to be cut is painful, and more than flesh and blood can bear.[4] And the woman who has this vice also is without a name; but she seems to be a conventional sort of woman.[5]

'It appears then that feminine courage is a kind of social virtue.[6] For women endure the fashions on account of the penalties arising from the customs and reproaches and honours.[7] There are, however, five spurious habits which are not truly courage, though in virtue of them many women will do brave things, and set many customs at defiance.

'Of these the woman brave from experience is most like the brave woman proper.[8] For having the eye from experience, she sees the many inanities of social life,[9] and being capable of using her dresses well, she knows best how to behave with a view to doing and not suffering,[10] and appears brave because the others do not know how things are.[11] But they are not truly brave, and show cowardice whenever the struggle grows too severe and they are left behind in the matter of dress and adornments,[12] like the

[1] Οὐ μὴν ἀλλὰ τὰ τοιαῦτα φοβήσεται, ὡς δεῖ δέ, καὶ ὅτε, καὶ οὗ, καὶ ὡς ὁ λόγος. Cp. *Eth. Nic.*, iii., 7, 2.

[2] This must be an allusion to a lost fragment of Plato's myth of the Lost Atlantis (cp. the *Critias*). There cannot be in it any prophetic anticipation of Chicago.

[3] Θρασυκακήν. This is a ἅπαξ λεγόμενον.

[4] Τὸ γὰρ κόπτεσθαι ἀλγεινόν, εἴπερ σάρκιναι, οὐδὲ ὑπομενητέον. Cp. *Eth. Nic.*, iii., 9, 3.

[5] Φαίνεται δὲ νομίμη τις.

[6] Πολιτική τις ἀρετὴ φαίνεται οὖσα.

[7] Cp. *Eth. Nic.*, iii., 8, 1.

[8] Τούτων μὲν οὖν ἡ δι' ἐμπειρίαν μάλιστα ὡμοίωται τῇ κυρίως.

[9] Ἔχουσα γὰρ ἐκ τῆς ἐμπειρίας τὸ ὄμμα τά τε πολλὰ κενὰ τοῦ πολιτικοῦ βίου συνορᾷ. Cp. *Eth. Nic.*, vi., 11, 7, and iii., 8, 6.

[10] Καὶ δυναμένη χρῆσθαι τοῖς πέπλοις, πῶς ἔχειν δεῖ πρὸς τὸ ποιῆσαι καὶ πρὸς τὸ μὴ παθεῖν κράτιστα οἶδεν. Cp. *Eth. Nic.*, iii., 8, 7.

[11] Cp. *ibid.*, iii., 8. 6.

[12] Ὅταν ὑπερτείνῃ ὁ ἀγὼν καὶ λείπωνται τοῖς πέπλοις καὶ ταῖς παρασκευαῖς. Cp. *Eth. Nic.*, iii., 8, 9.

Indian woman who went to the sacred festival thinking she would be the most beautifully arrayed, but finding that a richer was present, fled, casting away her arms.

'And very near to her comes she who thinks much of herself on account of good birth or wealth. For she also will do many things to please herself without loss of reputation, like Dido.[1]

'And further, she who acts in ignorance will appear brave without being so, as, for instance, the Milesian woman who asked the Great King to marry her, and when he said he was too old, apologised by saying she thought he was his son. The woman, however, mentioned above, who wears her jewels in a crowd, is not brave through ignorance, as some say, but truly virtuous. For she acts thus for the sake of the Beautiful (διὰ τὸ καλὸν), and all who do this are virtuous.

'Then too a woman when in love will do many brave things, and this form of courage seems to be most natural (φυσικωτάτη δ' ἔοικεν ἡ διὰ τὸν ἔρωτα εἶναι).[2] But she acts from emotion (πάθος) and not on account of the Beautiful, nor in accordance with the right proportion (κατὰ τὸν ὀρθὸν λόγον).

'Again, she who acts from shamelessness is not brave; since in that case Phryne was brave in the dicastery, and such things as they tell of French women (ἐπεὶ οὕτω γ' ἡ **Φρύνη** ἀνδρεία ἦν ἐν τῷ δικαστηρίῳ καὶ οἷάπερ, φασί, τὰς **Κ**έλτας).[3]

'Of feminine bravery then, let so much have been said, little indeed compared with the material which the subject affords, but much compared with what is seemly.'[4]

III.—Marriage.

The following fragment, which is clearly derived from the same source as the two former, seems to belong to the First Book of the *Ethics*. Prof. Susemeal has suggested that it should be inserted after the eleventh chapter, but in some respects it would fit in better before the tenth. It discusses the systematic position of Marriage in its bearings on **Εὐδαιμονία** with Aristotle's customary acuteness. In the traditional form of the *Ethics* this important subject is only just touched upon, and this fact alone would render the new fragment a welcome addition to Aristotle's masterpiece.

[1] The MSS. vary as to the spelling of the name, the best reading '*Dodo*,' and another '*Dado*'. The name itself is, of course, the same, being merely the feminine of Dōd (David).

[2] Cp. *Eth. Nic.*, iii., 8, 12. [3] Cp. *ibid.*, iii., 8, 11.

[4] Πρὸς μὲν τὴν ὑποκειμένην ὀλίγα, πρὸς δὲ τὴν εὐσχημοσύνην πολλά, supplying ὕλην rather than γυναῖκα with ὑποκειμένην.

'Next in order it follows to consider Marriage, not indeed in general—for that would belong to another and more painful inquiry, and we may assume such things as the mathematicians commonly prove concerning it, as that it requires *at least* two (*ἔστιν ἐν ἐλαχίστοις δυσίν*) and external goods and opportunity and the rest.

'But how it stands (*πῶς ἔχει*) in relation to Happiness it is fitting to consider, both for other reasons and because it is thought to be a good and to contribute not a little to Happiness. To many however, owing to the defect of human nature and the vicissitudes of fortune, it seems rather to be an evil, or at least disputable, so that it befits the prudent man to bethink him of the much quoted (*πολυθρυλητόν*) Solomonian Dictum—*Consider the end and call no man happy till he is divorced.*[1]

'But those who speak thus escape notice not speaking plainly. Do they speak thus of those who have obtained the Decree Absolute (*ἁπλῶς*) or the Decree *Nisi* (*τὸ εἰ μή*)? For these indeed rejoice, though not always according to right reason, if they are unmindful of the saying of Simonides,

'"There is many a slip 'twixt the cup and the lip,"

and the decree be not made absolute, but those suffer a strange thing (*ἄτοπον πάσχουσιν*) if they are called happy on account of a marriage which is already non-existent.

'And again, in respect to what are those divorced to be called happy? In respect to their past marriage or their present condition? If the one, is it not absurd to call them happy by reason of possessing what exists no longer; if the other, how are they happier than those who never married at all? But if any one quote Bias of Priene, correcting the saying of Theognis,

'"'Tis better to have loved and lost than never to have lost at all,"

he is defending a paradox.

'And again is it the past marriage or the divorce which constitutes the happiness of the divorced? Now if it be the divorce, it is impossible that a single action, however beautiful, should make a man happy, but only a firm habit of action. It is clear therefore that not one divorce is needed, but many, to attain this happiness, and that one divorce does

[1] Susemeal by excision of the sacred syllable OM emends this into 'Solonian,' though the MS. reading is quite clear. That Aristotle should thus show a knowledge of the Bible, and even of the Apocrypha, is no doubt surprising, but should only add to his reputation.

not make happiness any more than one swallow makes a drink.

'But if it be the past marriage, is it not strange to refuse to call a man happy then when he is happy, and to call him so when he is so no longer? It is clear then that if it can decently be done the happily married must be called so when they are married, and not when they are divorced.

'Shall we say then that their past marriage can contribute nothing to the happiness of the divorced? That indeed would be a very unkind doctrine (λίαν ἄφιλον) and contrary to opinions. But whatever influence reaches them must be very faint in their present condition, and not such as to control their happiness (ὥστε κύριον εἶναι).

'Or, again, did Solomon perhaps think that only when a marriage was dissolved could its happiness safely be estimated? In this indeed there is some speciousness, for there is great difficulty in establishing the happiness, or not, of a marriage. For it often happens that a marriage is at first happy and then turns to the reverse, even after many years, although the contrary of this hardly occurs. Wherefore, to one aiming at preciseness, it seems impossible to judge whether a marriage is happy or otherwise.

'In this respect indeed the unhappy marriage seems far better. For, as Socrates said, "an unhappy marriage one may find out in a day, but a happy one not in many years". Wherefore some contend that an unhappy marriage is both easier to achieve and more profitable, as being more knowable.

'Nevertheless it may be said that all these talk nonsense. For have we not shown that though Happiness must not be for a day or a honeymoon, but for a "complete" period, it need not be for ever? It follows therefore that it is not necessary to wait for a divorce before pronouncing a marriage happy or the reverse, but sufficient so to call it in a complete or perfect life (ἐν βιῷ τελείῳ). And so it is manifest that the happy man, possessing all the excellences and goods, will also be happily married during a perfect life. But nothing prevents the bad and imperfect from being unhappy in marriage. For it is possible that the intrinsically good is bad for the bad. In spite of their badness, however, though they cannot be perfectly happy, they can yet be perfectly miserable in marriage. And thus do they also attain the end.'

XI.—REALISM AND IDEALISM.

A MODERN PHILOSOPHICAL IDYLL.

BY VÉRA WELLDON.

STUFF with Nonsense took a stroll
To talk about the weather,
And they found that on the whole
They got on well together.

But presently—" My friend," says Stuff,
" I'm what all Mind is made of " ;
" Indeed," says Nonsense, in a huff,
" That's just what I'm afraid of !

" Make up your ' Mind ' then, if you please,
And let's have no more bluster,
For every man of Sense agrees
That Stuff's but filibuster."

" Oh, no," says Stuff, " a man of Sense
Calls you—not me—mere clatter,
For while you stand for nothing dense,
At least I stand for Matter."

" No Matter ! " Nonsense cries irate.
" For Mind is all we know of ;
It's full of me—at any rate
Enough to make a show of.

" But here comes Cousin Common-sense,
Who'll surely see me righted."
" Not he," says Stuff, " for in pretence
He beats us both united."

Yet both to him appeal at once
To read the mental riddle,
Each thought the other was the dunce—
The " stick " of folly's " fiddle ".

But, "Stuffed with Nonsense is man's head,"
Says Common-sense severely,
"And gingerly one has to tread
When nothing comes out clearly.

"Men credit others with a Mind
Of their own Nonsense 'eject';
No wonder animals—not blind—
Such powers of reasoning reject."

Whereon the two make friends again,
Dividing life between them,
To puzzle sore the wits of men
Who've talked, but never seen, them.

Now if this precious Stuff you've read,
Of Nonsense you'll be tired;
Pray write some Common-place instead,
For then you'll be admired.

XII.—AUS ZARATHUSTRA'S NACHLASS.

Mitgeteilt von "*Π*".

[How these papers escaped the vigilance of the Nietzsche Society and came to be contributed to Mind! would be an interesting tale, if it could be told. Their *cachet*, however, is unmistakable.—Ed.]

I. Vom Zahnschmerz und vom Übermenschen.

Als Zarathustra einmal in die Stadt zog, die zubenannt war 'die bunte Kuh,' stand auf dem Marktplatz ein Quacksalber und bot allerlei Zahnheilmittel feil. Das Volk drängte sich eifrig um ihn her, und am eifrigsten eine Alte, die schon lange keinen Zahn mehr im Munde hatte.

Da sprach Zarathustra zum Volke:—

Was glaubt ihr an Zahnschmerz und Zahnarzneimittel! Glauben und Aberglauben ist euer Leben. Was liegt aber an Zahn und Zahnweh? Der Übermensch wird kein Zahnweh bekommen: er soll dazu keine Zeit haben. Mit Zahnquacksalberei aber ist die Brücke zum Übermenschen nicht zu bauen: an Zahnschmerz könnt ihr nicht einmal untergehen!

Das Volk aber murrte und sagte:—

O Zarathustra, wir sind keine Übermenschen, sondern Alltagsmenschen, und Zahnweh ist einmal da. Wenn du uns nicht als Zahnarzt helfen willst, so ziehe deines Weges!

Da wendete sich Zarathustra zu seinem Adler und zu seiner Schlange und sprach:—

Wahrlich, meine Tiere, mit euch komme ich besser aus als mit jenem zahnverwesten Pöbel. Ohne Menschenzähne lebt ihr, stark, gesund und heiter, und fresst Frösche und Spatzen. Lauter Spatzen und Frösche sind die zahnschmerz-empfindlichen Kulturphilister. Euch aber würden sie nicht munden: denn sie sind zahm, und das echte Raubtier liebt nur Wildes. Also mögen sie sich in ihrem Sumpfleben aufzehren, bis auf den letzten hohlen Zahn! Erst dann lasse ich den Übermenschen kommen.

Also sprach Zarathustra.

II. Vom Diebstahl und vom Überhund.

Feuerrot sind meine Dachshündchen: schlangenartig ist ihr Leib. Weiss und scharf glänzen ihre Zähne: Zahnwehgetier sind sie nicht. Das Herz heiss wie's Feuer und den Kopf kühl wie die Schlange—so will ich den siegenden Held!

Man berichtet mir, sie haben ein Stück Fleisch gestohlen, und glaubt ich werde sie züchtigen. Das ist der 'Rechtsinn' der Gemeinen, wie ihn der Pöbel von seinen verehrten Weisen gelernt, diesen tugendlastertragenden Packeseln!

Ich aber lobe euch, meine Hündchen, dass ihr kühn und frech stehlt. Frech und offen wird auch der Übermensch Alles an sich reissen wozu er Lust hat. Stehlen aber wird er nicht können: denn im Reiche des Übermenschen soll es kein Gesetz mehr geben, kein Gericht, und kein Eigentum. Darin seid ihr dem Übermenschen selbst überlegen: denn Stehlen ist seliger als Nehmen. Heilig ist mir eure Tat: *Überhündchen* sollt ihr mir heissen.

Also sprach Zarathustra.

III. Vom Gepäck und vom Übermenschen.

Als Zarathustra aus Babylon fortreiste, hatte er einen Gepäckschein nötig. Den bekam er auch, und zwar in Keilschrift, wie sonst alle Propheten. Zarathustra aber, als Iranier und Gottloser, wollte von der semitischen, gottesdienstmässigen Priester-Kribbel-Krabbelkeilschrift gar nichts wissen. Als er den Schein nicht lesen konnte, ward er zornig und sprach zu seinen Jüngern:—

Schein und Gepäckschein! Was soll mir diese 'Hindeutung auf Sein'? Scheingötter und Scheinglaube und Scheingötterpack zur Schau tragen: das ist Sklavenmoral. Wahrlich, mir ekelt vor diesen scheinheiligen keilschriftgepäckscheinausstellenden Frommen!

Ich aber, Zarathustra, der gott- und gepäcklose, verkündige euch den gepäcklosen Übermenschen.

Kein Gepäck und keinen Schein wird der Übermensch brauchen: denn er soll als Gott tanzen, kleidlos und leidlos.

In der ewigen Wiederkunft soll er ewig gepäcklos tanzen, das Gepäck aber soll nicht wiederkommen.

Fort also mit dem Scheine!

Also sprach Zarathustra.

XIII.—ABSOLUTE IDEALISM.

By Hugh Leigh.

Absolute Thought! Grrr! Grrr!! Grrr!!! Absolute Rubbish! Bizz Ba Bosh! Ssss Bosh!! Ssss Bosh! * Pure Thought! * Pure Rot! * Hssk! Ssssk! Ssss!!! * I shiver! * Brr! Brrrrr!!! * Ow!!! * Lemme go! Lemme go!! Wa! Woe! Woo! Roo! * * * Beast! grrr! Swine! * * * Rrh! I wont! Razzle dazzle! razzle dazzle!! * I must! Zip! Rah! Boom! Siss! * I shall! Hip-rah-buss-sis! Sss!! Rah! Rah! Rah! Brahma!!! * * * Zip! Boom! Bang! I AM!!! Rah! Rah! Rah!, Rah! Rah! Rah!, Rah! Rah! Rah! Harvard! I'm Matter! Hah! Hah! Hah! Got im! Hah! Down! Yah! Yah! Yah! Cornell! I yell! To Hell! Cornell! Hum golly good! Ubble Bubble! Where's thought now! Rah! hah! Rah! hah! Rah! Gone! Rah! Rah! Rah! Gee Hugh! Jehu! Gee! Gee! Ee! Ee Hoo! Who! Hoo! lee! Hooley! Hooley! Loo! Hooley! loo! jah! Hugh Leigh!

'***YAH***!!!

At first we thought that this extraordinary production was a jumble of nonsense from a contributor who had suddenly gone mad over the study of Hegel. Next we thought it was a collection of the latest American 'College Yells'. Finally after great perplexities the truth dawned on us. It was a new and terribly effective criticism of Idealism by an appalling eruption of long-suppressed Matter. What Mr. Bradley had prophetically foreseen long ago had happened. The Irrational had revolted and its revolt was irreparable!

The mischief being done, it remained *only to understand it*, and so we thought it better to publish it, refraining from any comment, beyond printing Mr. Bradley's prophecy as the completest commentary on the situation.

"To the arguments urged by the reason, and which demonstrate that an element which is not intelligible is nothing, I possibly might not find an intelligible reply [*It hasn't*]. But I comfort my mind with the thought that if myself, when most truly myself, were pure intelligence, I at least am not likely to survive the discovery [*Nobody is!*], or be myself when I wake from a pleasant delusion. And perhaps it may stand with the philosopher's reason, as it stood with the sculptor who moulded the lion. *When in the reason's philosophy the rational appears dominant and sole possessor of the world* [italics ours], *we can only wonder what place would be left to it, if the element excluded might break through the charm of the magic circle, and, without growing rational, could find expression.*" [There would only be room inside, we fear, and, for a thought which has long been accustomed to absorb and transmute all things, the process of being itself gobbled up must be disgusting!] "Such an idea may be senseless, and such a thought may contradict itself" [Why not find out whether it does?], "but it serves to give voice to an obstinate instinct" [Which now seems to have got both voice and the upper hand!]. (*Principles of Logic*, pp. 532-533.)

ED., MIND!

XIV.—ZUR PHANOMENOLOGIE DES ABSOLUTEN UNSINNS.

Von Prof. Dr. G. W. Flegel.

Bekannterweise wurde es erst durch meine *Werke* auch dem philosophisch ungebildetsten Leser ermöglicht an der Entwicklung des *absoluten Wissens* teil zu nehmen und *den Gang der Sache selbst* ehrfurchtsvoll zu verfolgen. Nun aber geht die Sache der absoluten Philosophie leider schlecht, und seit einigen Jahren immer schlechter. Es wird dadurch zum Zweck und zur Pflicht des absoluten Geistes dieselbe wieder *auf die Beine* zu verhelfen, und zwar nicht dadurch dass er *die Ergebnisse der dialektischen Methode aufgibt*, sondern dadurch dass er dieselbe konsequent *fortsetzt*, und, indem er sich die heilsame Bewegung des *Sichselbstsetzens* macht, sich über alle die *sichselbstzersetzenden* Einwürfe der Andern unbeirrt *hinwegsetzt.* Nun *stellt* es sich merkwürdigerweise *heraus* dass diese *Fortsetzung* am *erfolgreichsten* am *Anfang erfolgt*, und in Folge dessen zugleich als *Voraussetzung* sich *vorstellt.* Mit andern Worten, der absolute Geist *stellt* sich am Anfang *vor* als die *absolute Voraussetzung seiner selbst* als dem *An und Für Sich* der reinen Vernunft der er *nachstellt.* Es dürfte aber bei dieser insichselbstzurückkehrenden *Bewegung* der reinen Vernunft Einem der Verstand *stille stehen*, und, da in Folge dessen der Geist *ausser sich* geriete, die Ansicht sich festsetzen, dass mit dem Absoluten *absolut Nichts* weder *anzufangen* noch *einzufangen* sei. Doch mit Nichten; denn dieser Anfang ist an sich abstrakt, und, wie alles raumzeitliche Geschehen, als solcher nur wesenloser Schein welchen die bewusstlose Faselei des sichselbstgleichen Selbstbewusstseins zum Ergötzen des zufälligen verworrenen und verwirrenden Bewusstseins seiner selbst erzeugt. Somit wird das in sich selbst reflektirte *Anheben* der dialektischen Bewegung keineswegs zu ihrem *Aufheben*, noch zum *Aufheben* ihrer Wahrheit; vielmehr ist *angehoben* nicht *aufgehoben*, noch *aufgehoben aufgeschoben*, und die *Wahrheit*, die gut *aufgehoben*, ist *aufbewahrt* und erst recht *wahr* und *bewährt.* Der als solcher sich ergebende Anfang der Bewegung ist also nur *aufgeschoben* oder vielmehr *zurückgeschoben*, indem sich die Vorstellung einer anfänglicheren Bewegung *vor ihm stellt*. Dem anfänglichem SEIN, welches sich im *Nicht-Sein* aufhob und im *Werden* vollendete, stellt sich also das DEIN vor, als das Anfänglichere. Noch *uranfänglicher* aber ist das MEIN, welches als der *absolute Anfangspunkt* (und daher auch *Endpunkt*) der Entwicklung des Geistes angesehen werden darf. *Meine Meinung* ist also kurz und bündig diese: Im Anfang ist Alles *mein*: das *Mein* schnappt indessen in das *Dein* über, welches, indem es sich entäussert, in das *Sein* übergeht, und dadurch den berühmten Gang der dialektischen Methode angeht. Dieser Anfang aber bildet zugleich den Beschluss der *Phänomenologie des absoluten Unsinns* und die Schädelstätte wo sich der absolute Geist den Kopf zerbrochen hat. Denn.

> "Nur aus dem Unsinn dieses Hegelreiches
> Schäumt ihm die Unsinnlichkeit."

XV.—PHOLISOPHY'S LAST WORD

(After a Woman's Last Word).

By I. M. Greening.

Grieved be thou no more, child,
  That to think
Leaves things as before, child;
  Only wink!

What so true as words are?
  True for me!
What so safe as girds are
  Up a tree?

See the sages stalking
  With their cleek;
Listen to their talking,
  Tongue in cheek!

When the leaves are drowning
  Let them rot;
When the nut is browning
  Crack it not.

Ware fresh fruit of knowledge
  To admit,
Lest they share thy college,
  Eve and it.

Be a god and bid me
  Banish sense;
Be a man and rid me
  Of pretence.

Teach, but not too clearly,
  This great Thought,
That the World is merely
  One plus *Nought*.

Duty means transcending
  Good and Ill;
Certainty pretending
  What you will.

Leave Kant, Hegel, Schelling
  To their night;
Nietzsche is more telling
  Out of sight.

Who said "What a bore," child?
  Gracious me!
When MIND! hits life's core, child,
  And truth's key!

XVI.—THE EQUIPMENT AND MANAGEMENT OF A MODERN ORACLE.

By Ursus Spelæus (Americanus).

To give good advice, said Schopenhauer, is easy; to take it, hard; to cease taking it, impossible. He infers that we had better give up giving and take to taking it. But as he does not tell us what is to induce us to take it, his advice is not practical. It is also *uneconomical* and unworthy of the commercial age we live in. For why should one *give* what is *worth* much money, and, when properly *brought* before the public, will *fetch* it? That the public pays generously and even greedily for *bad* advice is shown by its patronage of sporting prophets and stock-exchange tipsters. It may reasonably be conjectured, therefore, that it would pay still more for *really good* advice, if it were presented to it in a sufficiently attractive and impressive form. To effect this and many other laudable objects a Syndicate called the *Mind! Association* has recently been formed, which incontestably offers an attractive investment to persons endowed with capital and imagination.

It proposes to resuscitate an ancient, famous and well-tried method of getting people to take advice (on strictly cash terms), which, with the modern mechanical improvements it is intended to introduce, should prove simply irresistible. In other words the *Mind! Association* has obtained from the Greek Government a concession for the famous and beautiful island of Delos and has resolved to establish thereon a First-Class Oracle. An abridged prospectus of the Delian Oracle Co., giving full information as to the commercial aspects of the scheme, will be found at the end of this article: its present aim is only to explain the methods which open out to a Modern Oracle the prospect of a most beneficent, influential and profitable career.

In the first place it cannot be too strongly emphasised that the advice given by the Oracle will be good. Even if it should not in the first instance *appear* good, the Oracle will soon be in a position to *make it good.* To enable it to give good advice, to make it good, and to keep it good, no expense or trouble will be spared. The Oracle will retain the services of the highest professional talent from the prophet and clairvoyant down to the doctor and mechanician, and the possession of the best information on all subjects interesting to mankind will enable it to give the best advice with regard to them. In modern times both the collection and the transmission of such information have been so greatly facilitated that the Delian Oracle will be in a position easily to transcend the greatest achievements (in this line) of its forerunners and competitors. We have the men, we have the money, the only thing we still need is the organisation. And that the Delian Oracle will supply!

In order to avoid misconception it will be necessary next to define the position of the Oracle with regard to *Prophecy*. The Oracle will not of course disdain to prophesy when necessary, to avail itself of all trustworthy sources of prophetic information, or to use the appropriate methods of making its prophecies come true. On the contrary it will collect, collate and concentrate the prophetic material which now exists in a scattered form, and employ on its staff the most efficient prophets that love or money can procure. But its Directors do not intend to substitute Prophecy for Good Advice as the staple product of the Oracle, but to keep it strictly subsidiary. To know the future is valuable only if it enables men to act rightly, and it is this doctrine which the deliverances of the Oracle will enforce. Again, knowledge of the future is much commoner than the sense to use it, and so it will be the latter which by preference the Oracle will supply. Moreover the Directors are keenly alive to the fact that Prophecy is and has been, for the most part, in an utterly unregulated, uncritical and chaotic condition, and consequently quite untrustworthy. They infer that what the subject requires is systematic schooling, and hence propose to establish in connexion with the Oracle a scientific *School of the Prophets*, the syllabus of which will be found below.

With regard to *Miracles* the Oracle will preserve a similar attitude. They will not be performed wholesale. To do so would only vulgarise them and destroy their impressiveness. It would also be demoralising and discourage self-help. Moreover trivial miracles on trivial occasions are undignified. At the same time if a suitable occasion should arise, the Oracle will be thoroughly equipped to take advantage of it. Again with the mechanical and other improvements of modern times the results should infinitely surpass those of antiquity.

The *Consultation Fees* which the Oracle will demand will

be on a scale proportionate to the magnificence of the whole installation. It is obvious from what has been said that the Oracle will have to ask, will ask, and will receive, high fees, and make large profits. In general the Oracle will be conducted on the principle of giving no credit but taking all it can. At the same time, in order to give all a chance of participating in its benefits, there will charitably be instituted certain festivals on which consultations will be given gratis to the poor. In connexion with this it will probably be necessary to have a lottery, in order to decide which of the applicants are to be admitted to the shrine.

But after all what will chiefly distinguish the Delian Oracle from all similar enterprises in the past will be the completeness and perfection of its mechanical equipment. The Directors recognise that the success of a modern science depends largely, if not wholly, on the elaboration of a technical terminology and the generous provision of instruments for a laboratory. What, for instance, would Experimental Psychology be without these? Similarly it was felt that *Oracular Science*, or *Mantic*, must retain a pseudoscientific aspect so long as it was not adequately provided in these respects. Hence the Board have sanctioned a liberal expenditure on the instruments and arrangements, the use of which will be clear from the following account of the normal mode of consultation.

On admission to the sanctuary the applicant for divine guidance will find himself in the great outer court or colonnade, liberally provided with *Doves*, *Sirens*[1] and *Pseudomants.* Having handed his name to the *Big Drum Recorder* by means of an *Autosilligraph*, he waits at a *Tilt Table* or in an *Irritation Chair* until the god announces his pleasure to receive him through the *Stentor bellows.* He is then subjected to careful anthropometric examination by means of (1) the *Plutometer* (after which he pays his fee, which is recorded in the *Prophetometer*),[2] (2) the *Pseudometer*, (3) the *Follimeter*, (4) the *Snoboscope.* Next the *Psychopomps* and their assistants convey him into the bath-room, where he is *purified* by *Bathometers* and *Hip Chronoscopes.* After this he is cast into the *Chamber of Horrors* and exposed to the *Horrorscopes.* He is then taken into the *Innermost Shrine* or *Cella*, where the *Pythia* sits on the *Sacred Tripod* over the exhalations of the *Prophetic Vein*, and is separated from her only by a *Listening Moral Law Screen.* The

[1] These did not originally belong to the worship of Apollo, but will be found both ornamental and useful.

[2] An improved form of the *Cash Register.*

Pythia having transmitted the god's advice, the *Chief Metrognome*, having cast it into gnomic form and added all the requisite metrical improvements, recites it to the client, who then withdraws reverently, and is left for a while to recover from his ordeal. He is given *Memory Drops* in order that he may rightly remember what he was told. He may enter the *Silent Room* and contemplate its *Mutoscopes*. He may penetrate into the *Dark Rooms* and *Secret Chambers* lavishly furnished with *Rheostats*, *Di rheostats*, and *Arcanographs*, and capable of being still further darkened. He may examine himself by means of the *Prospectoscopes*, *Oneiroscopes*, *Humbugometers*, or amuse himself by watching the play of the *Collidoscopes*. Finally he will issue from the temple to the music and the forking tunes of the *Decampimeter* and return to his usual avocations relieved in his mind and purse.

In addition to the instruments already mentioned the laboratories of the Oracle must have an electric and prophetic Power Supply, and will also be fully furnished with *Indirect Prevision Colour Mixers*, *Pantelevators* (for raising moral tones), *Fall Phonometers*, *Telephotometers* and other *Telephotographic Apparatus*, *Chronographs*, *Kymographs*, *Telæsthesiometers*, *Personometers*,[1] *Telestereoscopes*, *Olfactometers* of every sort, and *Semnophones*.

It need hardly be said, however, that the instruments thus grouped under various (non-)sense names are by no means exclusively (non-)sensational instruments. Instruction in the use of this whole apparatus will form part of the work of the *School of Prophets*, with a sketch of which this article may fitly conclude. Students will be admitted to the institution after examination in such propaideutic subjects as mechanics, prestidigitation, physics, physiology, psychology (general and experimental), hypnotism, psychical research, logic, ethics and metaphysics, and the ideal length of the course will be three years. It will readily be apprehended, however, that the time actually required will depend on the progress and proficiency of the pupils.

In the first year, the student's mind having been properly purified by *fizzemetics*[2] and exercised by *chopsylogisms*, the subjects studied will comprise the *Elements of Magic* and the usual forms of *Mantic* (*Necromantic*, etc.), special stress however being laid on *Onomantic*, *Semantic*, and *Oneiromantic*. The abler students should also find time for *oneirocritical* and *sortilogical* exercises. In the second year the chief

[1] Improved and more powerful *Sonometers*.
[2] The American spelling of *physametics*.—Ed.

subjects will be *Advanced Magic* (in Black and White), *Mishaptics*, *Heliostatics* and *Pseudoptics*. In the third year the course will conclude with instructions in *Synoptics*, *Ecstatics*, *Fascination*, *Geloiology* and the *Use of Semnophones*. Students will normally be expected to work at least ten hours a day, but bodily health will be preserved by the practice of *Corybantics*, *Semantics*, and other antics. Instruction will be free, but the Oracle will reserve to itself the right of retaining the services of any of the Graduates of its School of Prophets.

Prospectus.

THE DELIAN ORACLE CO. (LIMITED).

Capital.

£1,000,000

divided into

100,000 Six Per Cent. Preference Shares and

100,000 Extraordinary Shares,

of £5 each.

Directors.

I. N. Roads, Esq.—Chairman of *Utopia Unlimited* and Director of the *Afrodesian Exploration Co.*

I. Wink, Esq.—Sporting Prophet of *The Turf.*

A. Gideon, Esq.—Financial Tipster of *Good Words.*

Frank Marks, Esq.—City Editor of *The Bad Times.*

Nimium Carus, Esq.—Editor of *The Moneyist.*

U. Spelaeus, Esq., Director of the *Mind! Association*, and Apollo, of the *Olympian Deities Syndicate*, will join the Board after allotment, as representatives of the promoters.

Bankers.

Messrs. Cave & Tugwell.

Solicitors.

Messrs. Hazey & Fogg.

Kassandra Vivacia,	Pythia.
Zadkiel,	Major Prophet.
Calchas Diplomaticus,	Minor Prophet.

Messrs. Tiresias, Jeremiah, Mohammed and Carlyle have consented to act as the *Advisory Committee* in the Shades.

This Company has been formed to take over from the *Mind! Association* its rights as owners of the ISLAND OF DELOS, together with the extensive rights (including Mining Rights and Jurisdiction) granted to it by a CONCESSION from the Greek Government, which reserves to itself only the Suzerainty of the Island. The Company's purpose will be to refound and operate the once famous Delian Oracle of Apollo.

The Island of Delos, one of the smallest but loveliest of the Cyclades, is at present situated in the Greek Archipelago. But according to ancient tradition it was originally a FLOATING ISLAND, which was fastened by Zeus to the bottom of the Ægean with adamantine chains, in order that it might safely bear Leto, and she in her turn the twin deities subsequently celebrated as Apollo and Artemis.

Modern archæology has confirmed this, like so many other legends, and it has also been ascertained that in the course of ages these chains have been almost worn through. Hence Col. Boreham, R.E., the celebrated martinet, reports that he would have no difficulty in boring through them with his diamond drill, in which event the Island would, owing to its extraordinary specific levity, once more become a floating island.

In order that this, however, may be done to advantage, it would be necessary to devise machinery capable of navigating the Island safely and successfully. With the recent improvements of the *Steereoscope*, however, this difficulty may be said to have been overcome, and it will consequently be possible to transport the Island, either by tugs or winds, aided by auxiliary steam engines on the Island itself, to whatever part of the Mediterranean may seem most attractive and expedient. The Island will sail under the Greek flag, but will be registered as 100 A 1 at Lloyd's. It is intended in the first instance to anchor it off the Riviera during the season.

It is manifest that the novelty of its procedure together with its natural mobility, will give it incalculable attractions as a *health resort*.

Owing to its size, as compared even with the largest steamers, and its moderate rate of speed, its motion will, however, be no more sensible than that of the Earth itself, no fear of sea-sickness need be entertained, and even the most fastidious need not be alarmed lest they should be disturbed by the proximity of any *Cyclades*.

With regard to the remarkable *mineral resources* of the Island, on which the chief success of the Oracle and the Company must ultimately depend, the subjoined report of the well-known Mining Expert, Mr. D. O. M. Browne, M.E., C.E, M.I.C.E., is conclusive. He says:—

"*Amid the French excavations of the Temple of Apollo I discovered, within a few feet of the surface, a prophetic vein whose extraordinary richness may be gauged by the fact that it yielded upon assay no less than . . .*[1] *per cent. of the theoretically predicted maximum. . . . The Specific Levity of the Island I estimate at* ·0125, *which is ample to support the buildings contemplated, and indeed any other construction that can be put upon it. It is chiefly caused by the rich veins of desiccated Humour which permeate the whole structure of the Island, and become evident wherever you bore it. At the North end especially the deposits are so plentiful as to form a veritable* COMIC MINE, *the produce of which might be largely exported without sensibly upsetting the balance of the Island.*"

The Purchase Consideration is £500,000 in Extraordinary Shares, leaving the whole of the £500,000 Preference Shares available as working capital for the development of the Island.

It is proposed to erect a handsome marble Temple of Apollo over the Prophetic Vein, and to build or sell sites for a number of First-class Modern Hotels at suitable points on the Island.

At each side of the entrance to the Temple there will be a number of entrancing Side Shows for the performance of Corybantics, Sacred Dancing, etc., the rental of which will add to the income of the Company.

The Directors have concluded a provisional contract of a very advantageous character with the Company operating the tables at Monte Carlo, affording them a refuge on the Island and a site for a branch establishment, which, in the event of trouble with the Prince of Monaco, would be converted into the chief centre of their business. To obviate, however, any moral exception that may possibly be taken to this arrangement, the Directors beg to announce that the Oracle will systematically discountenance the proceedings of the gaming tables, and refuse, on principle, to prophesy the lucky numbers of the day.

Negotiations are proceeding with a view to establishing an *Asylum for Sceptics*, for whose cure by Suggestion the Island will afford unequalled facilities.

The Directors are at present considering applications for licences from the Society of Select Sirens and the Amalga-

[1] For fear of European complications the Directors consider it advisable to withhold the actual figures. They will, however, be communicated in confidence to *bona fide* shareholders.

mated Herd of Harpies. Provision has already been made for high-class Centaur-Racing and Golf Lynx.

On the prospects of the political and financial influence which the Oracle seems likely to acquire the Directors consider it premature to enlarge. They do not, however, desire to conceal their conviction that eventually these may become the most important and remunerative parts of the Company's business.

The Company having obtained Apollo's *Patent Rights* and *Trade Secrets*, it is intended to establish *Branch Oracles* in suitable spots when and as they may be required.

N.B.—There is no duty on foreign oracles in the U.S. tariff.

It is evident that in some or all of these ways the Company will shortly find itself in the possession of a large and progressive income. Indeed the Dividend on its Preference Shares is ALREADY ASSURED, and they may therefore be regarded as a FIRST-CLASS INVESTMENT.

XVII.—THE M.A.P. HISTORY OF PHILOSOPHY.

RHYMES BEYOND REASON.

THIS important *History of Philosophy* is the fruit of long and anxious cogitation upon the proper method of teaching the subject. Its merits are novelty and conciseness. The Editors, however, neither guarantee the historical accuracy of the facts alluded to in these rhymes, nor hold themselves responsible for any of the opinions or sentiments expressed. Any one who has ever seriously tried to be a poet *knows* that all such matters are principally determined by the exigencies of rhyme. For the same reason we have had to omit many distinguished names which we should gladly have inserted, if it had been possible to obtain rhymes for them for love or money. The names of the persons concerned have been suppressed—for obvious reasons. They will be found however in the index.[1] Contributors to MIND ! have enjoyed the singular privilege of writing their own "Limericks," without being charged the usual advertisement rates.

The order is both chronological and logical.

I.—ANCIENT PHILOSOPHY.

1.

Though T—— held all things were water,
He married a wine merchant's daughter :
    From a corner in oil
    He gathered great spoil,
And routed the "City" with slaughter.

2.

"At one time," said A——,
"We sprang from a great Salamander,

[1] If not before.

Grew smoother and drier,
Democratic and higher,
Evolving a vast Gerrymander."

3.

H——, the Dark One,[1] declared—
"My damp sheets aren't properly aired,
The better is drier,
I swear by the Fire!
I'll give up my priesthood to C——!"[2]

4.

"I, sternly monistic, P——,
The Many consign to th' Eumenides,
All Being is One!"
"Yet, pardon the pun,
'Tis true you yourself are ¶ *many* D's!"

5.

A paradox crafty of Z——'s,
A cousin perplexed of Dan Leno's,
Cried he, "I'd no notion
There couldn't be motion!
I'll *go* to the Devil—p'raps he knows!"

6.

Young Z—— had only one notion—
To prove that there couldn't be Motion.
But his father said, "D——!
Why *solvitur am—*
bulando: go fetch me a potion!"

7.

When issuing **ΝΟΥΣ**! A——
Was asked: "Are you sage now, or wagorass?"
He replied: "Why of that,
'Tis as plain as my hat,
Man's the Measure. I hold with P——"

[1] ὁ σκοτεινός.
[2] "What does this mean?"—ED., MIND! "Don't you know that H—— was a High Priest and Master of the School of Prophets at Ephesus with the προεδρία and the scarlet gown?"—AUTHOR.

8.

"All's woeful and vain," said Heraclitus,[1]
"All's Atoms and Void," said D——.
"'Tis Matter for laughter,
'Gay Science' I'm after,
Or even a tale of Theocritus!"

9.

An accomplished Milesian A——
To Athens came over from Asia
Where she kept a *salon*,[2]
To her statesmen a boon,
And Perikles struck with aphasia.

10.

An idle old lounger was S——
(Though Plato a martyr the bloke rates);
When they asked "Is it sooth
You're corrupting the youth?"
"You clearly don't know 'em!" said S——[3]

11.

The divinest philosopher, P——,
Proved comforting very to Cato;
But our wiseacres laugh,
Immortality chaff,
And think him the smallest potato.

12.

An Asklepiad, great A——,
Felt terribly tempted to throttle
Alexander, his pup;
But they asked him to sup,
So he buried his wrath in a bottle.

[1] "Isn't the 'ī' long?"—Ed., Mind! "No—shortened by poetic licence."—Author. "Won't do; must draw the line somewhere. I shall draw it over the eye. You must try again."—Ed., Mind! "All right—How's this?

"With fooling one must meet men's folly—
D—— found it quite jolly;
In Atoms and Void
He really enjoyed
Specifics against melancholy."—Author.

"That will do much better, thank you."—Ed., Mind!

[2] We have, *of course*, changed our contributor's (presumably American) spelling '*saloon*,' in deference to universal historical tradition.—Ed.

[3] "Is this a fact?"—Ed., Mind! "Yes, on the authority of a recent examination paper, in which I found it almost *verbatim*!"—Author.

13.

We hedonists, said A——,
Discomforts detest when they grip us,
    So wealth we adore,
    The moment live for,
And take what the rich *'Arries tip us.*

14.

E——, famed master of swine,
Bred some pigs that (like Horace) were fine:
    But the pig that was taken
    And turned into B——
Came quite of a different line.

15.

Archie M——, with lever and screw,
Tried raising this planet a few:
    But he soon cried "Hallo!
    Where on Earth's my ποῦ στῶ?
They told me I couldn't: it's true!"

16.

A Stoic and slave, E——,
With courtesy ventured to greet us:
    But his master, enraged,
    In prison him caged
And told us to go, or he'd beat us!

17.

Said the paragon Emperor, M——,
"On ponderings let us embark us,
    All virtues we'll borrow,
    Take thought for the morrow,
The world cannot fail to remark us".

18.

The great thaumaturge, A——,
A wonder contrived so felonious,
    That they bade him globe-trot—
    Cried the sage, "This is rot!
For surely I *look* sanctimonious!"

19.

When Cyril met lovely H——
He shouted, "Come, lemme embrace yer!"
    She cried, "Get away, monk!
    You clearly are quite drunk!"
And abandoned the city for Asia.

20.

Of Egypt's weird wisdom Great T——
The mysteries showed me on oath,
Neith's Image unveiled,
Ra's Boat with me sailed :
Such secrets to tell you I'm loth !

21.

Life's Struggle than thou, Z——,
Who pictures us finer or vaster ?
Poetic and true,
I marvel thy view
The world has not managed to master !

22.

The infinite self-absorbed B——.
Was dreaming the World-Panorama ;
He groaned and he snored,
Till at length he grew bored,
And woke up, and broke up the Drama.

23.

O V——, Preserver Eternal,
Of Evil I deem you the kernel,
For if good and evil
You are, you're the Devil,
And the world you preserve is infernal !

24.

O V——, Preserver Eternal
Of all worlds, however 'external,'
Why were you a boar ?[1]
Why are you no more ?
Don't you think that the bore is eternal ?

25.

Of India's *Trimurti* dark S——
I fear was the gayest deceiver ;
He carried off *Maya*,
And made her his *ayah ;*
So people refused to receive her.

26.

A famous Scholastic, named A——,
Quite morbidly every tabby barred ;
Cried the Canon, " What's that ?
I'll *give* him the cat ! "
And terribly hurt him, the blaggyard !

[1] One of his most popular impersonations.

27.

Said Tom, the great Saint of A——,
"*Theology's Sum* is what we know,
My creed is scholastic,
God's very elastic,
Don't dare to expect that of *me!* No!"

28.

The *Doctor Subtilis*, old D——,
A Scotsman addicted to puns,
Maintained the Haecceity
Of Man and the Deity;
On fast days he lived upon buns.

29.

"To multiply beings," said O——,
"Is needless, 'tis better to dock 'em!"
So he seized on his razor,
This pestilent phraser,
And ran out to bloodily block 'em.[1]

30.

A Frenchman, whose name was D——,
Enlarged Geometrical Art,
His X, Y, and Z,
Although he's long dead,
Still play a most prominent part.

31.

A pestilent Jew, named S——,
To Yahveh put many a poser,
Till he went to the Hague
And died of the plague;[2]
Nowadays he'd have gone to Arosa.

32.

Thought the wily Lord Chancellor B——,
Whose faith in old methods was shaken,
"I'll simply set to
And start things anew
On the path that Posterity's taken!"

[1] "Don't understand. O——'s razor—yes: to 'block' razors, also; but why 'bloodily'?"—Ed., Mind! "To cut off their *blockheads*, of course! You also need it."—Author.

[2] "Surely S—— died of *consumption*, did he not?"—Ed., Mind! "Yes, that is why he would have gone to Arosa."—Author. "But you say he died of the plague."—Ed., Mind! "That is because he died at the Hague."—Author. "It's very puzzling."—Ed. "All the rhyme."—Author.

33.

With his mythical monsters old H——
Gave his readers some terrible jobs;
Now they've put on Hobbs Locke,
At Behemoths they mock,
And jeer at Leviathan's sobs.

34.

Now this is the legend of L——,
Of Christ Church a Student and *hock;*
On primary Matter
He did not grow fatter;
But dealt at innateness a knock.

35.

Sir Isaac, our chroniclers say,
Slept under an apple all day;
When it fell on his nose,
And disturbed his repose,
"Gravitation!" he shouted, "Hooray!"

36.

High-minded was good Bishop B——,
Through Matter he saw his God darkly:
His notions of Vision
Excited derision,
And multitudes stared at him starkly.

37.

A canny old Scotchman was H——,
Of dogmas he sounded the doom;
They call him a sceptic,
His thought's antiseptic,
In 'answers' there isn't a boom.

38.

'Twixt Monads, Herr L——, you see,
Communion can't possibly be:
You are one; so am I,
So it's useless to try
To fathom your "*Philosophie*".

39.

A German philosopher, L——,
Said one thing that's rather impressing:
"To hunt than to hold
Truth is, I make bold
To reckon, the far greater blessing".

40.

A Prussian professor named K——,
Proposed to his own maiden aunt;
Cried she in a huff:
"I've heard quite enough!
What, marry you? Nonsense! I shan't!"[1]

41.

Das Ich mit dem Nicht-Ich sich F——
Besah einst bei unsicherm Lichte;
Er rief: "Das Ich setzt sich!
Unding! Es entsetzt mich!
Das Ich macht das Nicht-Ich zu Nichte!"

42.

A German professor named S——
His doctrines proved simply *by yelling;*
He shouted aloud,
And attracted a crowd,
When questioned, he'd say: "That is telling!"

43.

Als berühmter Professor noch H——
Mit Begriffen oft spielte er Kegel;
Ihn erblickt' die Idee
Und rief aus "O Herr Je!
Ist *das* H——? Was ist das ein Flegel!"

44.

Sir Peter P. Pullinger, Bart.,
Abandoned his wife for his art.
But she found him again,
Manifestly insane,
As a German Professor called Her Bart.

45.

A pessimist, great S——,
Found living exceedingly sour,
At Hegel he cursed,
His grievances nursed,
And poured forth his wrath by the hour.

[1] "Surely this is not historical?"—Ed., Mind! "Not altogether. She really uttered only two words—the rest is poetical licence."—Author. "What were they?"—Ed. "*Anti-Kant!* See? Can *you* see what *Aunty can't?*"—Author.

46.

Nowadays it is held that a lot
Of the P—— theology's rot;
Though at Cambridge still read,
It may be called dead,
While Palae-ontology's not.

47.

"Than worship a wicked God," M——
Said, "in Hell I would far rather grill!"
But tutors like joking,
And fun at him poking;
They worry his poor old bones *still*.

48.

Great D—— shows Man, by his shape,
Is sprung from an Anthropoid Ape;
Though you needn't believe
That Adam and Eve
Had tails, they'd a narrow escape!

49.

Now Balliol's great Master was J——,
Quite plainly the anecdotes show it:
"Do well and succeed
Comes first in my creed,
No failures for me, if I know it".

50.

To deepen our consciousness G——
At Oxford appeared on the scene:
"O thinker obscure,
Why don't you make sure
That you know what you think that you mean?"

51.

The latest 'immoralist,' N——,
A very poor sort of a creature,
Was morbidly vain
And wholly insane,
A lunatic posing as preacher.

XVIII. — "ELIZABETH'S" VISITS TO PHILOSOPHERS.

By L. in her Grin.

I.

Königsberg, *Monday*.

Dearest Mamma,

I am sure you will be pleased to hear that we have safely got to the end of our horridly long journey this evening at seven, and that I am to call on the Great Philosopher to-morrow, armed with the letter which the Minister of Education, Herr von Zedlitz, very kindly gave me at Harry's request, when we stayed a day at Berlin. I did so hate the idea of going away to visit all these strange old philosophers in order to be cured of my giddiness and taught to be more serious, but you know what a good daughter I am, and how unlike most in these days and how dutifully I always do what you tell me, and mind you don't forget to give me those pearls you promised me if I would try to become wise and serious like the Owl of Minerva, or whoever it was. And really, dearest Mother, now that I am here I quite like the idea, and think it, Oh, such fun! For in its way it is quite as *risqué* and unconventional as anything I have ever done on my other visits, and I am quite excited about it and have to keep on telling myself that to the pure all things are pure. Because they're not, you know, but it's much more amusing if you make believe.

Nothing much happened to me on the journey except that Minister von Zedlitz said that he deserved a kiss for giving me the introduction (the idea! and he so fat and beery too!), and that the engine-driver asked me whether any one had ever run away with me on an express engine. But these are trifles and one gets so used to that sort of thing from men that no really nice girl minds it a bit. And the engine-driver was quite nice, except for the grease. So no more to-night from

Your ever affectionate daughter,

Elizabeth.

II.

Tuesday.

DEAREST MAMMA,

So I have been to see the great philosopher Kant, and I am sure I have done him a lot of good, though I am not so sure that he has me. I told Agnès to put out my blue dress, which you know is not very stunning, for fear lest he should be frightened, and drove to his house a little before three. His manservant opened the door and bowed deep when I handed him the Minister's letter all stuck over with big seals, and I was ushered into the sitting-room, or rather study, all covered with books and papers, but otherwise very neat. The professor had, it seems, been dozing in his arm-chair (he says he gets up at five every morning, can you imagine?), but got up and said he was honoured by my visit. Such a funny little hunchback he is, about five foot nothing, with such a big head and big bright blue eyes, and a blue coat and brass buttons. I told him I was Elizabeth. "*Ach ja, Elisabeth!*" he said, and his eyes filled with tears. Do you suppose, Mamma, that he once loved a girl called Elizabeth and that that is why he isn't married yet,—he must be quite old? Then I told him why I had come at your request, to be steadied by him because he was the greatest teacher of morals there was, and how innocent I was and how anxious to know all about his philosophy.

And he looked at me quite seriously and began telling, Oh, such a lot! I don't think I have got it quite clear, but I remember his beginning by telling me that such a form as mine did not come from his experience, though he was glad it came in it, and that it began in the experience of the happiest day of his life, and that he desired to cultivate the pure intuition (*reine Anschauung*) of me constantly, which he said was quite possible, because Space and Time were not real but transcendentally ideal. Then he went on to say a great deal about pure conceptions and categories. It made me feel quite queer and faint, but I think I've remembered most of the words. What he said about the Scheming of the Categories and their transatlantic deduction I did not quite follow, and the anti-monies I thought too stupid (don't you, Mamma, nowadays?), but what he said about the necessity of our having a Sympathetic Unity of Perception was quite charming. "But," I said, "how about the Categorical Imperative?" You remember you told me to ask about that particularly. Well, that stopped him, and I thought he was going to have a fit like poor Jean at Croixmare.

"*Ach ja,*" he stammered at last, "I had forgotten that and the pure respect I owe it." So I asked him what it was. "It demands," he said solemnly, "that thou shalt (don't you think, Mamma, that sounds quite too familiar?) not——"

At this point his old servant came in, his name is Lampe, and he carried his umbrella, and asked *ob denn der Herr Professor heute nicht ausgehen wollen*. It appears that the professor always goes out for an hour's walk at three every afternoon, so punctually that all the astronomers always observe his appearance and fix the time by him. And by this time it was ten past three by my watch.

"No," said the little man quite angrily, "*Lampe, scher' er sich zum Teufel, und lass er uns ungestört.*" Poor old Lampe withdrew quite crestfallen. So, to resume the subject, I asked him again what the Categorical Imperative demanded. "Thou shalt do thy Duty with no regard to inclination." "But what is my duty?" "To do as the Moral Law commands." "But what does the Moral Law command?" "The pure fulfilment of Duty." "But is not that what you said before and I could not make out? Can't you tell me more clearly?" He looked at me so earnestly that I nearly laughed, and then he grasped my hand and said, "Elizabeth, I will tell thee. Thy duty . . . thy duty is . . . to marry me!"

I know it was awfully rude, but really could not help it—I burst out laughing to his face. He seemed terribly hurt, so I said hastily: "But really, my dear good Professor, it is quite impossible, don't you see that you are quite 160 years older than me?" "Elizabeth," said he, "that makes nothing (*das macht Nichts*); have I not proved to thee and all the world that Time, though phenomenally real, is transcendentally ideal? Now, I love not only thy phenomenal appearance, I grant thee, but thy Noumenal Reality as a Thing-in-itself." This was too much. "Professor," said I, and I think I blushed, Mamma—it feels quite nice, "I am not accustomed to be spoken to like this; moreover, I think you ought to know that I am betrothed to the Marquis of Valmond, and so could not marry you even if you were a man who respected the decencies of polite language." And so I rushed out of the room and left him. But now that I come to think it over, I can't help feeling a little sorry for him. Do you think, Mamma, he really meant all he said? Anyhow I think I had better try some of the others first before I ask him again. So to-morrow we go back to Berlin to see Hegel, whom it will be quite safe to visit, because he is a married man and very respectable.

Your affectionate daughter,

ELIZABETH.

III.

BERLIN, *Thursday.*

DEAREST MAMMA,

I have just come back from my visit to Hegel, who is a *pigdog*, quite the worst I have met even in Germany. You shall hear. I had put on that dream of a dress you gave me last month, because I had heard this professor was quite fashionable, but when I was shown into the sitting-room by a thin care-worn little woman who had answered the door (she turned out to be his *wife!*) how do you suppose I found him dressed? In a dirty old flowered dressing-gown with a skull cap and a long pipe. At first he hardly seemed to notice me. I had to find my own seat (as at Kant's). I told him who I was, but he only said, "Yes, yes," and then shouted out, "Barbara!" The little woman came in trembling. "Barbara, pull off my boots and bring me my slippers." She had to kneel down and do it. While she was away, I asked why he treated her so barbarously. "She is my wife, you know," he said, "and the only woman who ever pretended to be logical. But *I* am a great logical reformer, and so I have to keep her in order, and sometimes to discipline her pretty severely." Still I don't think it at all nice, do you? Then he told her to get some coffee, and when she had brought it (he never offered me any, the pig!), told her she might go, which she submissively did. Then he asked what I wanted. I said I thought he could tell me the truth. "The Absolute Truth, I suppose you mean, for I keep no other." "Yes," said I, "that will do very nicely."

And then he told me. Oh, Mamma, it was terrible, and my head still aches merely to think of it. Of course I didn't understand a word: it was hard enough to look intelligent and appreciative in the right places. I can only remember that it began with the Absolute Nothing and ended with the most Absolute Non-Sense, and that it was all quite proper and very dull.

When he had done I asked him whether he did that sort of thing often. "Every day," he said "I lecture thus or nearly as well." "But don't you find it rather tiring?" "A little perhaps, because they none of them understand me. But the less they understand the more they admire, and I like that." "Then you should come over to England and go to Oxford," said I. He looked at me long with a cunning twinkle in his eye and then he said deliberately: "You are right, Elizabeth. I am tired of reforming Barbara, and of respectability and the Prussian State. You shall come with me and we'll start over again in Oxford. Thou alone, Elizabeth, art worthy of a logical reformer's true love."

I was so astonished that I allowed him to take my hand. "But," I said at length, "we should have to go by Hamburg and at Hamburg they have the cholera, while we are every day expecting the plague in England." "Cholera! plague!" he shrieked; "I live in terror of such things! I am feeling quite bad already!" And he turned quite pale. "Barbara! bring me a pill!" At this point I thought it best to withdraw, as he did not seem at all fit for any further rational conversation. But I do think him a pig, and poor little Kant was ever so much nicer. Now good-night.

Your affectionate daughter,

ELIZABETH.

PS.—*Friday* morning. Isn't it shocking, Mamma, I have just read in the paper the sudden death last night *from cholera* of the famous Prof. Dr. Hegel? Do you suppose it was funk, or do you think that Barbara put something into his coffee? I can't help thinking it must have been that, for I am sure she hated him, and no wonder. But how lucky for me he did not offer me any!

IV.

ATHENS.

DEAREST MAMMA,

I've been slumming! You said you would never let me try it, and now you have sent me there yourself. But of course when I went to see Socrates I had no idea they were so poor and had all to live in so small a hut. There are six of them, he and Xanthippe and four children, but desperately poor. Xanthippe, who is quite nice really, but terribly worried, because she says her husband won't work and she can't keep the whole family on nothing, was alone at home (the children were playing in the street) when I came in, and I felt very sorry for her and gave her all the money I had about me. So she cried and told me all about her troubles, how Socrates is the worst possible husband and father, and how shamefully he neglects them. And besides he drinks, not that he ever gets drunk, for he can stand any amount.

After a while Socrates came in and said he was pleased to see me. It was nice, because, though he was quite accustomed to young men coming to seek him out, Athenian girls were kept shut up so. Then he began by asking me whether I had ever been in love, and when I blushed and said I did not know, he said how charming I was and with what great pleasure he would help me deliver myself of the truth on this subject. And so he went on asking me questions about what I thought of the different kinds of love, all very queer, and things I didn't half understand. You know how innocent I am, but I am sure that most of what he said was improper. At last I could stand it no longer: so I told him outright I did not wonder that he got himself suspected as a corrupter of youth and I would hear no more.

So I walked off before he could stop me; but I think him a horrid man and so ugly too. Indeed, Mamma, I think the married philosophers are worse than the others, and so I had better go back to the unmarried ones, don't you think?

Good-bye, dear Mamma, with love from

Your affectionate

ELIZABETH.

V.

CORINTH.

DEAREST MAMMA,

Such a splendid place! And such a strange man! You might have told me what Mr. Diogenes was like, because when I arrived to-day and was shown into (do you say "into," Mamma?—because it wasn't) his tub and found him lying in a dirty wooden thing, I laughed out loud—and it would have been rude if he hadn't been asleep. He just rolled out all dirty and shaggy and gaped (such teeth, Mamma!) and said "Ah! stand out (yawn) my sun". So absurd! Because it was as dull as could be, and I said straight out: "There isn't any". He was quite amazed; and he gaped at me (such a gaby he is, Mamma!) and began to feel about in his tub and pulled out a plucked fowl. I had been thinking there was a very queer smell, but was afraid it might seem rude to remark on it. He held it out by the neck, horrid creature, and said: "Plato's man, the 'featherless biped'!" and laughed so loud. He must be a little mad, don't you think, Mamma? So I just said: "I don't understand you at all". And he stammered and said: "Oh, ah, er—I'm expected to say these things, you know. My reputation, you know." So silly, because no one you would like me to know has such things. Then he actually squatted down in his horrible tub and turned his back on me. I'm sure no Englishman would do that; and he growled out, "I've conquered pleasure," and I was so disgusted, Mamma, because none of the best people would ever think of doing that, that I said sharply: "What a silly thing to do". He shifted a little and I saw he was looking at me out of the corners of his eyes. "Socrates was a fool," he growled. "He has got a house," said I. "He visited Diotima" (do you spell it like that, Mamma? of course you know her). And then the horrible people began to laugh. "And a greater than Diotima is here," he said, and he squirmed round in his tub and looked up at me with such an *oily* smile. And the people giggled so that I was quite uncomfortable, and said, "It's very good of you," and I felt so stupid. He has big muscles in his arms and all over, only I do hate men with beards.

I tried to remember what you told me, Mamma, so I asked him what he had learnt from his studies, and he answered in jerks at once as if he was wound up: "To be able—to endure—my own company". And the silly people clapped. It seems that is what he always says, Mamma; so I asked him if it was hard, and he said, "Oh—ah—er—" just like before, and he looked so uncomfortable that I said I expected it was, just to help him out. And I was wondering what I ought to say next, because I'm not used to talking to a man in his tub, Mamma, when he cried out, "Give me—madness—rather than—pleasure," in the same jerks, and they said a sort of "Hear, hear!" So I said I was afraid I couldn't give him either, and I asked him if he could teach me anything else. That puzzled him again, and he squirmed about in his tub and said at last, "All that any man could teach you". And I told him I had nothing to learn from men; I wanted to learn from a philosopher. He cried out, "Is not the philosopher a man?" and I said I had no reason to think so. Then he actually stood up and took my hand in his dirty fingers and said, "Share my wisdom and my tub!" I was so astonished, Mamma, that I could only giggle and say you didn't approve of mixed bathing. And then his beard got quite bristly and he screamed, "Elizabeth, the philosopher does not wash"; and I said I had guessed that and managed to get away. But if that is the way the philosophers propose in Corinth, Mamma, I think they've neglected their opportunities for education. Corinth itself is a lovely place, something like Paris, but I didn't think the girls nearly as pretty as I had been told. And they didn't dress as much as *Parisiennes.* I do think men exaggerate frightfully about some sorts of girls. But I saw some nice-looking men in the town—only mademoiselle wouldn't let me stop. Good-bye, dearest Mamma.

Your affectionate daughter,

ELIZABETH.

VI.

WEIMAR.

DEAREST MAMMA,

Whom do you suppose I have visited to-day? You'll never guess, so I may as well tell you. I've called on Frau Schopenhauer, the novelist (not that I can read German novels, I think French are ever so much nicer and so instructive!), and got myself introduced to her son Arthur, the great pessimist. He was looking very grumpy, but he soon cheered up when I talked to him. He thinks life is not worth living, and we ought all to starve ourselves or at least desire nothing and be as humble and meek as the Christian Saints. Isn't he too funny? Not that he is at all like that himself really, but they say he has a terrible temper and is a *perfectly awful* woman hater. But he was very amusing all the same, and I fancy he rather liked me, for he said he would call at the hotel to-morrow afternoon.

Later.—I hardly feel equal, dearest Mamma, to telling you all that has happened since I began this letter. For I am really feeling quite upset and as you see my hand is still trembling. But I am quite sure that that Schopenhauer is either a brute or a madman and I can't think what would have happened if I had not managed to ring the bell. He was perfectly furious and I nearly fainted after he was gone, though you know, dearest Mamma, that I was never brought up to do anything of the sort. Anyhow you may be sure of one thing and that is that I will never go on a visit to another philosopher. The idea of sending innocent girls to them to become less frivolous! Why they are quite as bad as ordinary people, if not worse! Only their manners are ever so much worse, and they haven't the slightest appreciation of dress. On thinking it over, I know this will be a great disappointment to you, so we will compromise on this— I won't visit any more philosophers on my own to whom I have not been regularly introduced by you (you don't know any I am pretty sure!). Besides Valmond will be getting into mischief if I stay away from him much longer, and Lady Cecilia wrote me that odious Mrs. Smith was after him again. So I shall have to come back and box the ears of one or both of them again! So you may expect soon to be kissed by your affectionate daughter,

ELIZABETH.

VII.

THE MITRE, OXFORD.

DEAREST MAMMA,

You will hardly believe me after my last letter when I say I have been to visit another philosopher after all! And a very annoying and disappointing visit it was too, though quite different from any of the others. But the fact was that I felt that I had been writing you such perfectly *sweet* letters, and got so much good 'copy' (as those horrid pressmen call it), that I really must publish them somewhere. You know my other letters about my visits to fashionable people have been selling by thousands and are bringing me in heaps of money. And though we are rich you know that money is a thing one can never have too much of. And even though of course not so many people are interested in those silly old philosophers as in smart people I thought my name would enable me to turn an honest penny. So I wrote a little note to the dear old Archbishop of Canterbury and asked him what was the leading philosophic paper and when he told me it was MIND! I asked his son (whom I met at the Eights) where the Editor lived. It appeared that he lived at Corpus, a dear little out-of-the-way college you have probably never been to, and that he lived over the gateway. I thought the porter looked *just a little* surprised when I walked straight up and into the rooms. Fortunately he was in. Although I had been told he was called the Cave-Bear, he seemed quite pleased to see me, though a little embarrassed at first, until I told him I was Elizabeth. Then he smiled and said it had been his good fortune to owe much to Elizabeths. For instance the ornamental ceiling in his room had been put in in honour of Elizabeth. "What," I cried, "of that horrid old bore with the German Garden?" (He has beautiful rooms, but so dusty, which he says is the fault of his scout. But why doesn't he get dear Baden Powell's *Aids to Scouting* and make him read that?) Well, it seems that it wasn't that Elizabeth at all, but the stupid old queen I used to have to read about at school in the history books, who used to make all the young men at court flirt with her, which I thought most unfair.

Just then there was a knock and a man in a flaming tie burst in—and when he saw me he gasped and said, "Oh—ah—I beg your pardon," and slammed the door, and the Editor ran after him and called, "Mr. Smith," and I heard a voice choking with laughter say, "No—I—I—it's all right," and soon afterwards they seemed so merry in the quad, I wanted to look out.

However he was very pleasant about my letters and said he would be delighted to publish them in MIND! Then he made me some tea (which was good) and some puns (which were bad) and altogether was so nice that I thought he was going to be nicer still. In fact, I think he is the only one of all these philosophers whom I have visited who seemed to be what could possibly be called a gentleman.

But, and here comes the matter which made my visit such a disappointment, it is a humiliating confession to make, that *he never proposed to me* or said anything even remotely tending in that direction! It was not that I did not lead up to it, indeed I almost told him that that was what all nice men were expected to do. But I was afraid he might think it rude. So I only asked him what he thought of *Love's Dynamics*, and he replied he was no mathematician, but that if I was, I should probably need also to study the *Hydrostatics of Grief*, and finally I inquired what modern philosophers thought about the import of the proposal. "You mean, I suppose, of the proposition," he replied, and as I was weak enough to agree, I had as a punishment to listen to a little lecture on what he assured me was moderation logic. If that is logic in moderation, excess in it must be the most detestable thing in the world! And all the time I was wondering why he behaved so differently from the rest and didn't propose! Wasn't he stupid? Can you understand it, dearest Mamma? I can't[1] and I wish you would explain it to me! Else I shall be beginning to think there is something in that silly old philosophy after all. At least I will if I ever meet another philosopher like that. But it's very puzzling and makes me tired. So good-bye, dearest Mamma, for to-day.

Your affectionate

ELIZABETH.

PS. You needn't be alarmed about my becoming philosophic. When I am Marchioness of Valmond I shall never meet another philosopher!

[1] [I can.—ED., MIND!]

XIX.—A COMMENTARY ON THE SNARK.

By Snarkophilus Snobbs.

It is a recognised maxim of literary ethics that none but the dead can deserve a commentary, seeing that they can no longer either explain themselves or perturb the explanations of those who devote themselves to the congenial, and frequently not unprofitable, task of making plain what was previously obscure, and profound what was previously plain. Hence it is easily understood that the demise of the late lamented Lewis Carroll has opened a superb field to the labours of the critical commentator, and that the classical beauties of the two *Alices* are not likely long to remain unprovided with those aids to comprehension which the cultivated reader so greatly needs.

The purpose of the present article, however, is a more ambitious one. Most of Lewis Carroll's non-mathematical writings are such that even the dullest of grown-ups can detect, more or less vaguely, their import; but the *Hunting of the Snark* may be said to have hitherto baffled the adult understanding. It is to lovers of Lewis Carroll what *Sordello* is to lovers of Robert Browning, or *The Shaving of Shagpat* to Meredithians. In other words, it has frequently been considered magnificent but not sense. The author himself anticipated the possibility of such criticism and defends himself against it in his preface, by appealing to the 'strong moral purpose' of his poem, to the arithmetical principles it inculcates, to 'its noble teachings in Natural History'. But prefatory explanations are rightly disregarded by the public, and it must be admitted that in Lewis Carroll's case they do but little to elucidate the *Mystery of the Snark*, which, it has been calculated,[1] has been responsible for 49½ per cent. of the cases of insanity and nervous breakdown which have occurred during the last ten years.

It is clear then that a Commentary on the *Hunting of the Snark* is the greatest desideratum of English Literature

[1] See the Colney Hatch *Contributions to Sociology* for 1899, p. 983.

at present; and this the author of the present essay flatters himself that he has provided. Not that he would wish the commentary itself to be regarded as exhaustive or as anything more than a *vindemiatio prima* of so fruitful a subject: but he would distinctly advance the claim to have discovered the key to the real meaning and philosophical significance of this most remarkable product of human imagination.

What then is the meaning of the *Snark?* Or that we may not appear to beg the question let us first ask—how do we know that the *Snark* has a meaning? The answer is simple; Lewis Carroll assures us that it not only has a meaning but even a moral purpose. Hence we may proceed with his assurance and our own.

I will not weary you with an autobiographical narrative of the way in which I discovered the solution of the Snark's mystery; suffice it to say that insight came to me suddenly, as unto Buddha under the Bô-tree, as I was sitting under an Arrowroot in a western prairie. The theory of the Snark which I then excogitated has stood the test of time, and of a voyage across the Atlantic, in the course of which I was more than tempted to throw overboard all my most cherished convictions, and I have little doubt that when you have heard my evidence you will share my belief.

I shall begin by stating the general argument of the Snark and proceed to support it by detailed comment. In the briefest possible manner, then, I assert that the Snark is the Absolute, dear to pholisophers, and that the hunting of the Snark is the pursuit of the Absolute. Even as thus barely stated the theory all but carries instantaneous conviction; it is infinitely more probable than that the Snark should be an electioneering device or a treatise on "society" or a poetical narrative of the discovery of America, to instance a few of the fatuous suggestions with which I have been deluged since I began to inquire into the subject. But further considerations will easily raise the antecedent probability that the Snark is the Absolute to certainty. The Absolute, as I venture to remark for the benefit of any unpholisophical enough still to enjoy that ignorance thereof which is bliss, is a fiction which is supposed to do for pholisophers everything they can't do for themselves. It performs the same functions in philosophy as infinity in mathematics; when in doubt you send for the Absolute; if something is impossible for us, it is *therefore* possible for the Absolute; what is nonsense to us is *therefore* sense to the Absolute and *vice versa;* what we do not know, the Absolute knows; in short it is the apotheosis of topsyturvydom. Now

Lewis Carroll as a man of sense did not believe in the Absolute, but he recognised that it could best be dealt with in parables.

The *Hunting of the Snark*, therefore, is intended to describe Humanity in search of the Absolute, and to exhibit the vanity of the pursuit. For no one attains to the Absolute but the Baker, the miserable madman who has left his intelligence behind before embarking. And when he does find the Snark, it turns out to be a Boojum, and he 'softly and silently vanished away'. That is, the Absolute can be attained only by the loss of personality, which is merged in the Boojum. The Boojum is the Absolute, as the One which absorbs the Many, and danger of this is the 'moral purpose' whereof Lewis Carroll speaks so solemnly in his preface. Evidently we are expected to learn the lesson that the Snark will *always* turn out a Boojum, and the dramatic variety of the incidents only serves to lead up to this most thrilling and irreparable catastrophe.

But I proceed to establish this interpretation in detail. (1) We note that the poem has 8 fits. These clearly represent the Time-process in which the Absolute is supposed to be revealed, and at the same time hint that Life as a whole is a *Survival of the Fit.* But why 8 and not 7 or 9? Evidently because by revolving 8 through an angle of 90° it becomes the symbol for Infinity, which is often regarded as an equivalent of the Absolute. (2) The vessel clearly is Humanity and in the crew are represented various human activities by which it is supposed we may aspire to the Absolute. We may dwell a little on the significance of the various members of the crew. They are *ten* in number and severally described as a Bellman, a Butcher, a Banker, a Beaver, a Broker, a Barrister, a Bonnetmaker, a Billiard-marker, a Boots and a Baker. It is obvious that all these names begin with a 'B,' and somewhat remarkable that even the Snark turns out a Boojum. This surely indicates that we are here dealing with the most ultimate of all questions, *viz.*, 'to be or not to be,' and that it is answered in the universal affirmative—B at any cost!

Next let us inquire what these personages represent. In the leading figure, that of the *Bellman,* we easily recognise *Christianity,* the bell being the characteristically Christian implement, and the hegemony of humanity being equally obvious. Emboldened by this success, it is easy to make out that the *Butcher* is *Mohammedanism,* and the *Banker Judaism,* while the *Beaver* represents the aspirations of the animals towards τὸ θεῖον.[1] The anonymous *Baker* is, of course, the

[1] Cp. Aristotle, *Eth. Nich.*, vii., 13, 6.

hero of the story, and the "forty-two boxes all carefully packed with his name painted clearly on each" which he "left behind on the beach" typify the contents of his mind, which he lost before starting on his quest.

The *Barrister* is clearly the type of the *logician* and brought 'to arrange their disputes'. He too has dreams about the Absolute and wearies himself by proving in vain that the "Beaver's lacemaking was wrong"; as any one who has studied modern logic can testify, it does dream about the Absolute and is always 'proving in vain'.

The *Broker* brought 'to value their goods' (ἀγαθὰ) is evidently *moral philosophy*. The "*Billiard-marker* whose skill was immense" is certainly *Art*, which would grow too engrossing (= "might perhaps have won more than his share") but for the pecuniary considerations represented by the Banker (Judaism) who "had the whole of their cash in his care".

In the *Boots* we can hardly hesitate to recognise *Literature*, which serves to put literary polish upon the outer integuments of the other intellectual pursuits.

The *Bonnetmaker* finally is manifestly the *Fashion*, without which it would have been madness to embark upon so vast an undertaking.

Having thus satisfactorily accounted for the *dramatis personæ* I proceed to comment on the action.

F. 1, st. 1.

> "Just the place for a Snark the Bellman cried,
> As he landed his crew with care.
> Supporting each man on the top of the tide
> By a finger entwined in his hair."

The meaning evidently is that Christianity "touches the highest part of man and supports us from above".

F. 1, st. 12.

> "He would joke with hyenas."

It is well known that few animals have a keener sense of humour than hyenas and that no animal can raise a heartier laugh than the right sort of hyena.

> "And he once went a walk paw-in-paw with a bear."

The learned Prof. Grubwitz has discovered a characteristically Teutonic difficulty here. In his monumental commentary on the *Shaving of Shagpat*, he points out that *as human* the Baker had no paws and could not possibly therefore have offered a paw to a bear. Hence he infers that the text is corrupt. The "w" of the second "paw" is evidently, he thinks, due to the dittograph initial letter of the succeeding "with". The original "papa" having thus been corrupted into a "papaw" (a tropical tree not addicted to locomotion), an ingenious scribe inserted "w-in" giving a specious but mistaken meaning. The original reading was "papa with a bear," and indicates that a forebear or ancestor was intended. So far Grubwitz, who if he had been more familiar with English slang would doubtless have dealt with the text in a more forbearing and less overbearing manner. Anyhow the difficulty is gratuitous, for it must be admitted that the whole stanza is calculated to give any one paws.

"Just to keep up its spirits he said."

It was probably depressed because it could only make a bare living.

In the second Fit the first point of importance would seem to be the Bellman's map. This is manifestly intended for a description of the *Summum Bonum* or Absolute Good, which represents one of the favourite methods of attaining the Absolute. Moreover, as Aristotle shows, a knowledge of the *Summum Bonum* is of great value to humanity in crossing the ocean of life, although its *τέλος* is *οὐ γνῶσις ἀλλὰ πρᾶξις*.

F. 2, st. 2.
"What's the good of Mercators, North Poles and Equators,
Tropics, Zones and Meridian Lines?"

These terms evidently ridicule the attempt made in various ways to fill in the conception of the *Summum Bonum*, but I confess I cannot identify the chief philosophic notions in their geographical disguises.

F. 2, st. 6.
"When he cried 'Steer to starboard, but keep her head larboard!'
What on earth was the helmsman to do?"

The question in the first place is quite irrelevant, as the helmsman was not on earth but at sea and likely to remain there. Still, bearing in mind the effect of this remarkable nautical manœuvre, we may perhaps make bold to answer: "He should have turned tail!" For the effect upon the ship would be to make it toss and, as the Bellman obviously preferred the head, the helmsman should have cried "Tails!"

F. 2, st. 9.
"Yet at first the crew were not pleased with the view,
Which consisted of chasms and crags."

When Humanity first really catches a glimpse of the local habitation of the Absolute in the writings of the pholisophers, it is disappointed and appalled by its "chasms and crags," *i.e.*, the difficulties and obscurities of these authors' account.

F. 2, st. 10.

"The Bellman perceived that their spirits were low,
And repeated in musical tone
Some jokes he had kept for a season of woe,
But the crew would do nothing but groan."

Tutors have been known to adopt similar methods with a similar effect.

F. 2, st. 15. We now come to what is perhaps the most crucial point in our commentary, namely, "the five unmistakable marks, by which you may know, wheresoever you go, the warranted Genuine Snarks. Let us take them in order. The first is its taste, which is meagre and hollow but crisp; like a coat that is rather too tight in the waist with a flavour of Will-o'-the-Wisp."

1. The taste of the Snark is the taste for the Absolute, which is not emotionally satisfactory, 'meagre and hollow, but crisp' and hence attractive to the Baker, while the elusiveness of the Absolute sufficiently explains the 'flavour of Will-o'-the-wisp'. Its affinity for 'a coat that is rather too tight in the waist' applies only to its 'meagre and hollow' character; for unless the coat were hollow you could not get into it, while it would, of course, be meagre or scanty if if were 'too tight in the waist'.

2. "Its habit of getting up late you'll agree
That it carries too far when I say,
That it frequently breakfasts at five o'clock tea
And dines on the following day."

In this the poet shows, in four lines, what many pholisophers have vainly essayed to prove in as many volumes, namely that the Absolute is not, and cannot be, in Time.

3. "The third is its slowness in taking a jest.
Should you happen to venture on one,
It will sigh like a thing that is deeply distressed;
And it always looks grave at a pun."

This third characteristic of the Absolute is also found in many of its admirers, I am sorry to say. It is best passed over in silence, as our author says elsewhere, without "a shriek or a scream, scarcely even a howl or a groan".

4. "The fourth is its fondness for bathing-machines
Which it constantly carries about,
And believes that they add to the beauty of scenes,
A sentiment open to doubt."

The 'philosophic desperado' in pursuit of *Nirvana* achieves his fell design by a purificatory plunge into the ocean of Absolute Being. This, however, is not an æsthetic spectacle which 'adds to the beauty of scenes,' and hence the Snark obligingly carries bathing-machines about in order that in Mr. Gladstone's phrase "essential decency may be preserved".

5. "The fifth is ambition." The Snark's ambition is to become a Boojum, of course. It always succeeds with those who are prepared to meet it half-way. You will doubtless have noticed that the five unmistakable criteria of Snarkhood we have just considered are all of a spiritual character and throw no light upon its material appearance. The reason no doubt is that our author was aware of the Protean character of the Absolute's outward appearance, and with true scientific caution did not pretend to give an exhaustive description of the various species of Snark. What, however, he does know he is not loth to tell, and so he bids us distinguish "those that have feathers and bite from those that have whiskers and scratch". In this it is needless to seek for a causal connexion between the possession of feathers and mordant habits. The fact is simply mentioned to distinguish these snarks from birds which have feathers but—since the extinction of the *Archæopteryx* and *Hesperornis* —have long ceased to wear genuine teeth and to bite, and angels which have feathers but don't bite, not because they are physically, but because they are morally, incapable of so doing. Similarly it would be fanciful to connect the scratching, which is attributed to the second kind of Snark, with the possession of whiskers even in an inchoate condition. But *v. infra* for the doubt about the reading.

Let us consider therefore first the information about the outward characteristics of these snarks. Some have feathers, some have whiskers. There is no difficulty about the former. We simply compare the well-known Poem of Emerson on Brahma; in which the latter points out to those who object to being parts of the Absolute, that "when me they fly I am the wings". If wings, then probably feathers; for the featherless wings of insects are utterly unworthy of any kind of Snark.

The mention of snarks with whiskers on the other hand constitutes a difficulty. For we cannot attribute anything so anthropomorphic to the Absolute. There is, however, evidence of a various reading. The Bodleian MS. B$\frac{n}{2}$ 48971, which is supposed to be in the author's own handwriting, reads *whiskey* instead of *whiskers*. The change is a slight one, but significant. For we may then compare Spinoza's well-known views about the Absolute, which caused him to be euphemistically described as 'a God-intoxicated man'. It should also be remembered that various narcotics such as bhang, opium, hashish, arrack, etc., have been used to produce the mystic union of the devotee or debauchee with the Absolute, and many hold that whiskey is as good as any of them.

It remains to account for the habit of the Snark in biting and scratching. The learned Grubwitz, to whom allusion has already been made, thinks that these terms are intended to indicate respectively the male and female forms of the Snark (who, in his opinion, represents the university student who is capable of becoming a Boojum—a professor causing all who meet him "softly and silently to vanish away"). The demonstrable absurdity of his general theory of the Snark encourages me to reject also Grubwitz' interpretation in detail, in spite of my respect for his learning. I should prefer, therefore, to explain the biting and scratching more simply as due to the bad temper naturally engendered in so inordinately hunted an animal.

The Third Fit opens, as the reader will doubtless remember, with the attempts made to restore the fainting Baker.

"They roused him with muffins, they roused him with ice,
They roused him with mustard and cress,
They roused him with jam and judicious advice,
They set him conundrums to guess"

Such as, probably, *Riddles of the Sphinx*. The other means seem to have been injudicious.

Skipping, with the Bellman, the Baker's father and mother, we come to his "dear uncle," who, *lying* on his death-bed, was able to give the important information which has proved so epoch-making in the history of Snarkology.

And first let us ask who was the "dear uncle"? In answering this question we not only gratify our scientific curiosity but also discover the name of the Baker, our "hero unnamed," as he is subsequently (F. 8, st. 4) called. Now it must be admitted that we are not told the uncle's name either, but I think that from the account given there can be little doubt but that it ought to have been Hegel. Now a distinguished Oxford pholisopher has proved that what may be and ought to be, that ∴ is; and so the inference is practically certain.

F. 3, st. 7.

"He remarked to me then, said that mildest of men,
If your Snark be a Snark, that is right;

Fetch it home by all means—you may serve
It with greens"—T. H. Green's to wit—
"And it's handy for striking a light."

It is well known that Hegel thought that the *wrong* kind of Absolute (that of the other professors) was 'like the night in which all cows are black'. It follows that the right kind—his own—would conversely serve as an illuminant.

F. 3, st. 8.

"You may seek it with thimbles—and seek it with care,
You may hunt it with forks and hope,
You may threaten its life with a railway share,
You may charm it with smiles and soap."

"You may seek it with thimbles"—this passage is repeated in F. 4, st. 8, by the Bellman, whose subsequent remark in st. 10, "To rig yourselves out for the fight," explains its meaning. Evidently Lewis Carroll here meant subtly to suggest that the pursuit of the Absolute was a form of intellectual *thimble-rigging*.

"You may hunt it with forks and hope." Just as only the brave can deserve the fair, so only the *forktunate* can *hope* to attain the Absolute. There is no justification for depicting Care and Hope as allegorical females joining in the hunt, as the illustrator has done. Altogether the serious student cannot be too emphatically warned against this plausible impostor's pictures; they have neither historic authority nor philosophic profundity. He attributes, *e.g.*, a Semitic physiognomy to the Broker instead of to the Banker; he persistently represents the Baker as clean-shaven and bald, in spite of the statement (in F. 4, st. 11) that "The Baker with care combed his whiskers and hair," and his picture of the Snark exhibits neither feathers nor whiskers! "You may threaten its life with a railway share." This alludes to the deleterious effect of modern enlightenment and modern improvements on the vitality of the Absolute. "You may charm it with smiles and soap." *I.e.* adulation and ascetic practices, soap being the substance most abhorrent to Fakirs and Indian sages generally, and therefore suggesting the highest degree of asceticism.

But after all, the momentous revelation of the Baker's uncle is neither his account of the methods of hunting the Snark—they are commonplace enough and he evidently did not choose to divulge his own patent of the Dialectical Method—nor yet his account of the use to which the Absolute may be put—it is trivial enough in all conscience—but rather the possibility—nay, as in the light of subsequent events we must call it, the certainty—that the Snark is a Boojum. No wonder that even the dauntless Baker could not endure the thought that if he met with a Boojum he would "softly and suddenly vanish away," and that the Bellman "looked uffish and wrinkled his brow". He was of course bound to conceal his emotions and to take an uffishial view of the dilemma. So his reproaches are temperate—

"But surely, my man, when the voyage began
You might have suggested it then,
It's excessively awkward to mention it now."

". . . And the man they called Hi! replied, with a sigh,
I informed you the day we embarked—
I said it in Hebrew, I said it in Dutch,
I said it in German and Greek,
But I wholly forgot, and it vexes me much,
That English is what you speak."

The accounts of the Absolute in German and Greek are famous, while the Hebrew and Dutch probably both refer to Spinoza, who was a Dutch Jew, though he wrote in bad Latin. The forgetting to speak (and write) English is a common symptom in the pursuit of the Absolute.

F. 4, st. 13.

"While the Billiard-marker with quivering hand
Was chalking the tip of his nose."

Art, when brought face to face with the imminence of the Absolute, recoils upon itself.

The argument of the Fifth Fit is broadly this, that the Butcher and the Beaver both hit upon the same method of approaching the Absolute, by way of the higher mathematics, and so become reconciled. Into the reason of this coincidence, and the rationality of this method it boots not to inquire, the more so as it proved abortive, and neither of them were destined to discover the Snark. That they were brought together, however, by their common fear of the *Jubjub Bird* is interesting, and could doubtless be explained if we could determine the meaning of that volatile creature.

Let us ask, then, what is the Jubjub? In reply I shall dismiss, with the brevity which is the soul both of wit and contempt, the preposterous suggestion that the Jubjub is the Pelican. But I am free to confess that I have spent many a sleepless night over the Jubjub. Philologically indeed it was not difficult to discover that Jubjub is a 'portmanteau bird,' compounded of 'jabber' and 'jujube,' but even this did not seem at first to give much of a clue to the problem. Finally, however, it struck me that the author had, with the true prescience and generosity of genius, himself stated the solution of the riddle in the line immediately preceding his description of the Jubjub. It is—

"Would have caused quite a thrill in Society".

It flashed across me that the Jubjub was Society itself, and if I may quote the account of the Jubjub's habits it will be seen how perfectly this solution covers the facts.

"As to temper the Jubjub's a desperate bird
Since it lives in perpetual passion."

This describes the desperate struggle and rush which prevails in Society.

"Its taste in costume is entirely absurd,
It is ages ahead of the fashion."

How profoundly true this is! To be in Society this is what we must aim at; we can never be in fashion unless we are ahead of the fashion.

"But it knows any friend it has met *once* before."

It is most important in Society to remember the people you have met even once, alike whether you intend to recognise them or to cut them; otherwise vexatious mistakes will occur. There is subtle sarcasm also in the use of the term 'friend' to describe such chance acquaintances.

"It never will look at a bribe."

Such is its anxiety to pocket it.

"And in charity-meetings it stands at the door
And collects, though it does not subscribe."

No one who has ever had anything to do with charity-bazaars can fail to recognise this!

"Its flavour when cooked is more exquisite far
Than mutton or oysters or eggs."

The taste for Society is of all the most engrossing.

"Some think it keeps best in an ivory jar
And some in mahogany kegs."

Some think Society appears to best advantage in an ivory jar, *i.e.*, a 'crush' of *décolletées* women, others at a dinner party over the mahogany board.

"You boil it in sawdust; you salt it in glue."

Dust is American slang for money, so 'sawdust' is put *metri gratia* for 'sordid-dust'. That is, Society is boiled, *i.e.*, raised to the effervescence of the greatest excitement, by filthy lucre. "You salt it in glue." 'Salt' is short for 'to captivate by putting salt on its tail,' 'glue' is put metaphorically for 'adhesiveness,' and the whole, therefore, means that Society is captured by pertinacity.

"You condense it with locusts and tape."

I.e., lest it should become too thin, you thicken it with parasitic 'diners out' to amuse it, and officials (addicted to red tape) to lend it solemnity.

"Still keeping one principal object in view,
To preserve its symmetrical shape."

The importance of keeping the proper 'form' of Society intact is too obvious to need comment. It is hardly necessary to add also that the reluctance of the Mohammedan and the animal to face a society in which the female sex dominates to such an extent fully explains their common fear of the Jubjub. Lastly it is clear that a word compounded of jabber and jujubes, the latter being used metaphorically for all unwholesome delights, Turkish and otherwise, is a very judicious description of Society.

The Sixth Fit is occupied with the interlude of the Barrister's dream, which seems to have been prophetic in character and throws further light on the Absolute. That Logic should dream of the Absolute will not of course surprise those who have followed the recent aberrations of the subject. Let us consider then this dream of Logic's.

F. 6, st. 3.

"He dreamed that he stood in a shadowy Court,
Where the Snark with a glass in its eye,
Dressed in gown, bands and wig, was defending a pig
On the charge of deserting its sty."

The pig was probably *Epicuri de grege porcus*, and the charge of deserting its sty was a charge of pig-sticking or *suicide*. For, as the divine Plato excellently shows in the *Phædo* (62 B), to commit suicide is to desert one's post, and so to desert the *four* posts of the pigsty must be still worse.

F. 6, st. 4.

"The Witnesses proved, without error or flaw,
That the sty was deserted when found,
And the Judge kept explaining the state of the law
In a soft undercurrent of sound."

The Judge is *Conscience*, the exponent of the Moral Law, noted for its still small voice.

F. 6, st. 6.

"The Jury had each formed a different view,
Long before the indictment was read,
And they all spoke at once, so that none of them knew
One word that the others had said."

The Jury is *Public Opinion* which was evidently (as so often) very much perplexed by the pigculiarities of the case.

F. 6, st. 7.

"'You must know——' said the Judge; but the Snark exclaimed 'Fudge!'
'That statute is obsolete quite;
Let me tell you, my friends, the whole question depends
On an ancient manorial right.'"

The question was whether the pig was free, or *ascriptus haræ,* justly 'penned in its pen'. In other words, does being born involve a moral obligation to remain alive?

F. 6, st. 8.

"In the matter of Treason the pig would appear.
To have aided but scarcely abetted."

For a soldier to desert his post is, or may be, treason hence the charge of treason against the suicide.

"While the charge of Insolvency fails, it is clear,
If you grant the plea 'never indebted'."

The suicide is accused of insolvency, of failing to meet the obligations which life imposes on him. His reply is 'never indebted,' he owes life nothing, he received no 'stipend' and will not be 'sued for a debt he never did contract'.

F. 6, st. 9.

"The fact of Desertion I will not dispute,
But its guilt, as I trust, is removed
(So far as relates to the costs of this suit)
By the *Alibi* which has been proved."

You prove an *alibi* by not being there. The pig's defence was that it was not there or not all there, in other words, not *compos mentis.* That is, the old excuse of temporary insanity!

F. 6, st. 10.

"But the Judge said he never had summed up before,
So the Snark undertook it instead."

Conscience has to pronounce judgment upon the particular case, but this particular case has never occurred before; hence Conscience finds itself unable to decide and leaves the matter to the Absolute. The attitude of Public Opinion is similar, "when the verdict was called for the Jury declined," and "ventured to hope that the Snark wouldn't mind undertaking that duty as well".

In the end the Absolute not only has to defend the offender and take his guilt upon Itself, but also, as ἓν καὶ πᾶν, to assume all the other functions as well, to find the verdict and to pronounce the sentence. Its readiness to do this is suspicious, and suggests the idea that it was acting collusively throughout in pretending to defend the pig.

"So the Snark *found* the verdict," *where* we are not told, but *what* we might have anticipated.

> "When it said the word GUILTY, the Jury all groaned
> And some of them fainted away."

The verdict involved a shock to enlightened Public Opinion, like that of the Dreyfus case. The sentence after that seemed comparatively light and so was received with approval.

> "'Transportation for life,' was the sentence it gave,
> 'And then to be fined forty pound.'
> The Jury all cheered, though the Judge said he feared
> That the phrase was not legally sound."

The sentence was of course absurd, for the suicide had already transported himself out of jurisdiction.

F. 6, st. 15.

> "But their wild exultation was suddenly checked
> When the JAILER informed them with tears,
> Such a sentence would have not the slightest effect
> As the pig had been dead for some years."

The JAILER, whose duty it is to keep the pigs in their styes, is the *doctor*. After all, you can do nothing with a *successful* suicide.

F. 6, st. 16.

> "The Judge left the Court looking deeply disgusted:
> But the Snark, though a little aghast,
> As the lawyer to whom the defence was intrusted,
> Went bellowing on to the last."

Though such events shock the Conscience, the Absolute is unabashed.

The Seventh Fit is devoted to the Banker's fate and perhaps the most prophetic of any. For no discerning reader of this commentary can fail to recognise that it forecasts the encounter of Judaism with Anti-Semiticism. Let us follow the description of this disgraceful episode in contemporary history.

F. 7, st. 3.

"A Bandersnatch swiftly drew nigh
And grabbed at the Banker, who shrieked in despair
For he knew it was useless to fly.
He offered large discount—he offered a cheque
(Drawn to bearer) for seven-pounds-ten:
But the Bandersnatch merely extended its neck
And grabbed at the Banker again."

The Anti-Semitic Bandersnatch shows that it cannot be bribed by insufficient 'ransom,' and that two can play at a game of grab.

"Without rest or pause—while those frumious jaws
Went savagely snapping around,
He skipped and he hopped, and he floundered and flopped
Till fainting he fell to the ground."

After the Anti-Semitic rioters had been driven off, it was found that the Banker—

". . . was black in the face, and they scarcely could trace
The least likeness to what he had been:
While so great was his fright that his waistcoat turned white—
A wonderful thing to be seen!"

This alludes to the wonderful affinity Judaism has for clothing, and we may parallel this passage by referring to Shakespeare's (?) *Merchant of Venice*, Act ii., Scene 1. There an insult offered to his 'Jewish gaberdine' produces a powerful emotional effect upon Shylock. Here conversely the ill-treatment of their wearer calls forth a sympathetic compensatory effect on the part of the clothes.

In the Eighth Fit the Tragedy reaches its consummation and comment is almost needless.

It must be *read*, not without tears, and every line in it confirms the view we have taken of the Snark.

F. 8, st. 8.

"Erect and sublime, for one moment of time."

I.e., before becoming a moment in the timeless Absolute.

F. 8, st. 9.

"In the midst of the word he was trying to say,
In the midst of his laughter and glee,
He had softly and silently vanished away
For the Snark *was* a Boojum you see."

One can't help feeling a little sorry for the Baker personally, but nevertheless the verdict of Philosophy must be: "So perish all who brave the Snark again!"

XX.—THE M.A.P. HISTORY OF PHILOSOPHY.

II.—Modern Philosophy.

It may have occasioned some surprise to the readers of this History of Philosophy to find how far down the range of Ancient Philosophy has been extended. But a little reflexion will show them that the dividing line has been drawn in the only logical place, *viz.*, *between the dead and the living.* All defunct philosophers must necessarily be esteemed ancient philosophers, inasmuch as after death a philosopher at once falls a prey to commentators, is no longer able to speak for himself, and cannot be asked to explain what the d—— he meant. He has in short won his way to the inaccessible.

It is evident therefore that the distinction between the dead and the living is really the most important, not only for them, but also for us. Moreover (except for scientific purposes) a live lion is far more to be redoubted than *any number* of dead asses (be they as rare as quaggas!). And *a fortiori* the *live* asses are still more formidable. Recognising this we have thought it best to allow our living menagerie to raise its voice, each after its own kind.

The only objection that could fairly be brought against our scheme of classification is that it is not exhaustive, and does not provide for a third and most numerous class, that of the *dead-alive* philosophers. Indeed it has been speciously maintained, in Hegelian quarters, that these are the truest philosophers, constituting the higher synthesis of the antithesis between the dead and the living. But whatever speciousness certain facts may give to this doctrine, it is clear that this division will not serve the purposes of Mind! The aim of Mind! is to stimulate rather than to depress philosophic interest, and it must therefore proceed by anatomy and dichotomy. We have, however, by way of precaution, exacted an affidavit that he really is a live philosopher from all we proceed to celebrate.

52.

A learned professor called Smyth[1]
Said, "Of Wisdom I'll tell you the pith—
    Contradictions I find
    In the Absolute's Mind,
But believe in the Absolute'S myth".

53.

A staid Merton Fellow, named B——,
Fell in love with the Absolute madly;
    A big book he wrote
    Its perfections to note:
The Absolute looked at him, sadly.

54.

An excellent Master, called C——,
His beard so unfrequently pared,
    That it grew to such length,
    And imparted such strength
That no one to tackle him dared.

55.

If a man is what he eats,[2]
Living by cooking his meats—
(Absorb this, I pray, in your hookah),
    Then the Essence of Man,
    And his Strategy's plan,
Must plainly depend on 'the Cooker'.

56.

O Fairest Bairn, O Fairest Brother,
Is each one both, or each the other?
    On the Absolute musing
    Is very confusing:
Personality seems such a bother!

57.

"To amass erudition," said J——,
"Is poor fun: I've tried it and know it:
    But your son as a ruler[3]
    Can keep comfy and cooler,
On *a thousand a year*, Ma'am, and go it!"

[1] The reason for this apparent departure from our rule of anonymity is obvious. Smyth is not really a name; it is universal, not particular. It may therefore, as Aristotle says, be called *ὄνομα ἀόριστον*, as being applied to an infinite number.

[2] *Est quod est.*

[3] *I.e.* in the Civil Service.

58.

"But, Sir," said the mother to Joke him,
"There are better things"—this to provoke him—
"Perhaps you are right
To put it so, quite—
Two thousand a year will not choke him!"

59.

Herakleitos' loveliest daughter
Understood him (because he had taught her):
By her Flame and her Fire
She did men inspire,
And still she's inspiring B——.

60.

Of Platonists biggest, once B——
To Demeter offered a pig;
When they made him a light
In the place of old B——
The Pelican dancèd a jig.

61.

When S—— to Oxford repaired,
And Green's "incoherence" declared,
"Of course we can still
Go on, if we will,
To Hegel" (or Hades), said C——.

62.

Cried B—— "This is very Sidg-wicked!"
(Without him one cannot play cricket)
"Our bottom's knocked out,
For a Carpenter shout,
And board it up, lest they should kick it!"[1]

63.

New morals are taught by 'the R——,'
With Joseph's a bit of a clasher;

[1] "This looks as if it might be fun and even fact, if one could fathom it. Can't you explain? Is a *ball* or a *bat* the necessary instrument to see the joke withal in line 2? And is the Carpenter Alice's?"—Ed., Mind! "Both are sheer history and explain themselves. Note, however, that Hegel has proved that a bat is a bird and not a bird, whose synthesis is absorbed as a moment in the dialectical chase of the Wild Goose. *Per contra* the (Estlin) Carpenter adores the Pelican."—Author.

He's great as a writer,
Should rise to a mitre,
But never will shine as a masher.

64.

A Waynflete professor named C——,
Was great on the Aryan Race,
On the birch and the bark,
And the beech and the Snark
(Alas! I am wrong! It was S——!).

65.

The great Orientalist, S——,
Was stung by an asp in the face;
He knew all about cricket,
Thought idealists wicked
(Dear me! I am thinking of C——!).

66.

A man of both worlds is EN. B——.
Not only the newspapers ken it;
He follows the hosts,
Investigates ghosts,
And aspires to a seat in the Senate.

67.

Our Pedagogue, strenuous K——,
Has new ways to stop the boys cheating;
To fix their attention,
I need merely mention,
He lately gave each boy a beating!

68.

Now Exeter's Tutor is M——,
A man of nigh *twenty-five* carat,
No savage is he,
Though trying to be
(I can't get a rhyme for his merit!).

69.

An eloquent lecturer, B——,
Wished vainly his class would grow small;
Said he, "If it's true
They teach well who teach *few*,
They teach *best* who teach no one at all".

70.

Thomas F——, of Corpus, our "Pre,"
A gentle Logician is he,
His kindness and sense
Are simply immense,
For praises you may come to me!

71.

We have a *Wilde Reader* named S——,
Most learnedly ready to spout
Of birds, beasts and babes,
And eke astrolabes [1]—
There's nothing he knows not about!

72.

When the Absolute dreamt of a flea [2]
There sprang up a Tutor named L——
He worried It much,
The Annoyance grew such
That It cried, "I'll absorb him in Me!"

73.

An astute Ass^t. Tutor named S——,
Of MIND!'s Essence the subtle distiller,
Above Corpus gate
Jokes early and late,
While the Pelican grins on her pillar.

74.

Our excellent friend, Henry S——,
With æsthetics was anxious to flirt,
Of Dons, Babes and Duty
He found out the Beauty,
And urged us to put on a spurt.[3]

75.

Reformer and Cricketer K——,[4]
At Greenness he wittily mocks;

[1] "What sort of beasts are these?"—ED., MIND! "Poetical licence for psycho-physiological instruments in general!"—AUTHOR.

[2] Cp. *Riddles of the Sphinx*, p. 353.

[3] As Editor of a forthcoming (?) volume of Philosophical Essays.

[4] [On receiving this description of our esteemed contributor we at once wired to the Author: "Are you not confounding the persons? John K— and F. P. K— are *not* the same. How many K—es are there, and which do you mean, anyway?" Weeks afterwards came this haughty reply, on a post-card: "Don't know and don't care! One or three, *au*

Of his work much you'll find
In this number of MIND!
Never mind if some fogies it shocks!

76.

At Manchester Sam A——
Conducted a new propaganda;
Cried he, when a goose
Approached with abuse,
"Away with you, improper gander!"

77.

Though hardly a moralist, T——
O'er perilous seas is a sailor,
He imitates B——,
And does it not badly,
Some think him at ethics a nailer.

78.

The greatest American J——
The Kantians call *other* names;
Let them say what they will,
We adhere to it still,
The Will to believe is Will J——.

79.

A Cambridge idealist, W——,
Relentlessly put to the sword
The naturalist crew,
Till they cried: "That will do!
Professor, you've certainly scored!"

80.

I'm Herbert the Sage, the De S——
Of truths that grow daily immenser,
My thought is synthetic,
Please take (with emetic!)—
In Collins' patent condenser.

81.

The Lady Victoria W——
Invented a method to spell by;

choix. What *does* it matter? Are they not *all one* in the Absolute? But see *Law Reports*, vol. xlix., p. 666."

On investigating this cryptic reference, we found only an account of a breach of promise case, "Howard *v.* Knox," the relevance of which we were unable to discover. It did not appear that our hero was in any way implicated.—ED., MIND!]

She taught us *Semantics*,
And other such antics,
Significance truly to tell by.

82.

Though a faithful disciple, McT——
His own master Hegel quite staggered;
For he said, with a chortle,
"I can prove I'm immortal,
Beat that if you can, you old braggart!"

83.

A mighty logician called V——
Soars frequently out of our ken,
His logic '*Symbolic*'
Don't try as a frolic;
With luck you may '*Chance*' it, but then!

84.

The great anthropologist, F——,
Writes wrapt in his toe-tems and blazer,
While over his brows
He wears *Golden Boughs*
He cut off at Rome with a razor.

85.

Though living at Florence, AW. B——
Retains a sharp point to his pen,
You'll find he makes jokes
And fun at fools pokes,
And cheers up the gods and the men.

86.

An excellent banker named C——
Denies the existence of God,
Prefers Herbert S——,
Thinks matter grows denser,
And will—till he's under the sod!

87.

At Yale, I was told by my dad,
The boys are all taught by a L——,
When they row in the boat,
'Tis *Scripture* they quote—
If the tale isn't true, it were sad.

88.

His name is the Latin for 'dear,'
His thoughts run on Science and Beer;
He edits the *Monist*,
I fancy he's honest,
But don't think they read him much here.

89.

The book of the *Wisdom of W——*,
Though written in Japanese slang,
Aroused Iba Sotaro
To mete out a deadly blow
To Hoshi Toru and his gang.[1]

90.

Said a Tutor of * * * [2], Doll,
"This doctrine I teach to my Coll.:
'Tis no matter what you *do*,
If your Truth [3] be only *true*".
And his truth was true—to Doll!

91.

A portly professor inclined
To think Matter a function of Mind:
Each day after dinner
He *thought* himself thinner,
No matter how well he had dined! [4]

92.

Another, who daily grew fatter,
Held Mind was a product of Matter,
Said he: "Mental growth
And bodily, both
Proceed from a well supplied platter".[3]

[1] *Wang-yang-ming*, the Japanese Kant, held that conscientious convictions must be acted on at all costs, as divinely inspired. Hence when Iba Sotaro felt convinced that Hoshi Toru's influence was evil, he felt it was his duty to assassinate him. And he did. See the *Times* (4th Oct.) for the whole story. It is hoped that a selection of the *Works of Wang* will shortly be published in *Mind*.

[2] "Of what, please?"—Ed., Mind! "Anything!"—Author.

[3] "How about this metre? And in the original 'his *heart* was true to Poll'."—Ed., Mind! "Bab Ballads!"—Author.

[4] "Who are these? Can't guess. Give more data."—Ed., Mind! "Leave it to you. The verses are universal—their application only is particular. Only be particular about the application!"—Author.

93.

Smith,[1] thinking to help the Ideal,
Spent his time proving Time was unreal,
Till he cried out "Sublime!
I'm sure I've *done* Time!"
"Why, what did you do? Did you steal?"

94.

An Oxonian, addicted to rhyme,
In his essays essayed to *save Time;*
When they gave him a *Third*
He exclaimed: "How absurd!
To have *killed* it was surely the crime!"

95.

A tale I tell to fill the world with grief
For Martyr Smith, and beggar all belief!
Not mine an idle mass of futile fictions,
But simple fact; he died of his convictions!
"Convictions? Heavens! Did some brutal Bench
Invoke the *chose jugée* in fashion French?
Was theft or treason of his crimes the chief?
(The good man Plato well has proved a thief[2])"
Ah, no! The fatal force that burst the links
'Twixt him and life was *Riddles of the Sphinx.*
Though not convicted, he was yet convinced
He'd floor a book at which his elders winced:
So, calling down a *judgment* on his pride,
He read one *sentence* and then promptly died!

96.

Von Deutschland's Denkern der Letzte,[3]
Im Himmel das Ding an Sich setzte
Doch der Teufel der kam,
Das Ding an Sich nahm,
Ihn hinterlings schändlich verletzte.

97.

Of maternal devotion, O Pelican,
Thou'rt symbol; but now, swears a Mexican,

[1] "What Smith again? What Smith?"—Ed., Mind! "Anysmith."—Author. "Lady Smith?"—Ed. "See *ad.*, No. 54, and if you don't like Smith, try Jones, or almost any monosyllabic philosopher."—Author.

[2] *Republic*, 334 A.

[3] "Who is this?"—Ed., Mind! "Can't bother to enlighten you. Why don't you read the German *Fachblätter?*"—Author.

When blind, *you* are fed
By your chicks till you're dead—
The story I fear is American.[1]

98.

My rhyme now arrives at I——,
An attribute dark of divinity;
That it rose out of Nought
But a misconceived Thought
Is a truth they should teach you at Trinity.

99.

Though aged and useless, The O——
In a race tried the Many to run,
Then the interest grew,
Till through wires there flew
The message: "The Many have O——".

100.

O Cussedness, Cosmic, Eternal,
Of Being the innermost kernel,
You're human, you're worse,
Universal, perverse;
I doubt not your work is infernal.

101.

And now let us hymn last the A——,
From It first did everything evolute;
If your mind you would lose,
You must stand in its shoes,
You'll find it a terrible Trapsolute!

L'Envoi.

Cried a Passman, who read this, "Great S——!
How *did* they compile all this rot?
Though clever they be,
I'm glad it's not me!
Philosophy! Nonsense, it's not!"

[1] See Darwin's *Descent of Man*, ch. iv.

XXI.—THE ABSOLUTE AT HOME.

By A Troglodyte.

A Tragedy

in

One Act (*Actus Purus*).

Dramatis Personæ.

The Absolute, absolutely at home.
Her Fossilliness The Universal, housekeeper to the Absolute.
The Father of Lies, *alter ego* to the Absolute.
Truth, a lovely maiden who has just come out.
Experience, a wise old teacher.
Inexperience, her sister.
Pholisophers, fools, fogies, pedants, categories, schemata, etc.

Scene I.

The Father of Lies. Hallo, who is this sitting by the well? A lovely girl, by Brahma, attractively disarrayed! I must accost her. (*Goes up to her.*) Who art thou, pretty one? What is thy name and of what parents wert thou born?

Truth. It is borne in on me that my name is Truth, but what I am I hardly know as yet. You see I have only just come out.

F. of L. Out of what?

T. Out of this well.

F. of L. You are well out of it! Ha ha! And of your parents?

T. I know nothing, save that I read on the notice-board that 'Truth is evolved out of Error by the immanent self-criticism of Experience'. But I know neither Error nor Experience.

F. of L. Then you must be as wholly *a priori* as you are charming. I am delighted too to find that we must be nearly related.

T. How?

F. of L. Why, I am not only well acquainted with Experience, but Error is indissolubly wedded to Falsehood, who is the offspring of Lies, of whom I boast myself to be the father!

T. I cannot follow the relation which, you say, results. It ought to be worked out on the notice-board. And in any case it seems to me that to be 'nearly related' is not to be really related. A miss is as good as a mile!

F. of L. (*Aside.*) How easily innocence is sophisticated in these days! (*Aloud.*) At all events you are not a miss, but a most egregious——

T. Sir, do you doubt my honour?

F. of L. (*Aside.*) Pulled up again! (*Aloud.*) You mistake me! I know you are a Miss in one sense, but in that I meant you are Nature's most stupendous hit, and do not come amiss to me!

T. You puzzle me, but if you mean well, you might tell me what I ought to do. You see, I do not know my way about the world as yet.

F. of L. (*Aside.*) Already she is trying to be practical! Really the Absolute and I must take steps to stop this pestilent growth of Pragmatism. (*Aloud.*) I will see that you are properly launched upon the world. Come with me now and be introduced.

T. To whom?

F. of L. To everybody.

T. Where are you going?

F. of L. To the Absolute's, which is At Home to-day. So the whole world will be there and the half as well. It will be a great lark, for as Hesiod says 'the half is more than the whole'.

T. What half?

F. of L. The better half of course! (I must not yet shock her!) The Universal too will be charmed to meet you.

T. What are the Absolute and the Universal.

F. of L. *Sancta simplicitas!* What is the Absolute! Why everything! I can't possibly explain It. You must take It on trust. But the pholisophers all say that It is absolutely real. However I dare say, though It is at home to-day, you will soon find It out for yourself. (*Aside.*) I did long ago, but I always find it pays to praise It to others. (*Aloud.*) As for the Universal, there is a great deal I might tell you about her.

T. Pray tell me.

F. of L. In the first place she's the Absolute's housekeeper, and people do say a good deal more. But why should I

8

corrupt your innocent mind with the vile slanders of those who cannot see that to the profound all things are profound, and that a mystery and a deity can be made out of the most unpromising materials, if only you keep them dark enough? Let it suffice you that without her the Absolute can or will do nothing, and that she receives all Its guests.

T. I am surprised that people go.

F. of L. Oh, one must not be too particular. Especially about the Universal. Besides, everybody has to go.

T. I cannot.

F. of L. Nonsense! Why not?

T. You see how little of a dress I have for such a function.

F. of L. Oh, that doesn't matter. The Absolute will like you, will address you and, I dare say, still think you overdressed.

T. I don't like your account of the Absolute at all. And how about the Universal?

F. of L. Oh, Her Fossilliness will mind still less. You see she isn't particular and indeed can't afford to be so.

T. But why do you call her 'Her Fossilliness'? What does it mean?

F. of L. It's a little pet name I gave her, because the pholisophers haven't yet found out how stupid she really is. But come you *must*, it's your chance and you ought to think yourself lucky.

T. I suppose I must, but I never dreamt of becoming a 'necessary truth' so soon. [*Exeunt.*

SCENE II.

A crowded reception at the Absolute's Home, commanding a fine view out of Space and Time.

EXPERIENCE AND INEXPERIENCE.

Inexperience. Do you know, sister, who the lovely girl was that old Father of Lies was taking into the Reception Room to be presented? She seemed to me to be the realisation of all one's ideals of Beauty, Truth and Goodness in one.

Experience. I feel sure that was Truth, though I can never quite make out whether she is three or one. I have never seen her here before.

In. It seems a pity that she should be sacrificed to the Absolute.

Exp. A burning shame. But I see no way to stop it, so long as the pholisophers approve of whatever happens to be traditional, and will not listen to me.

In. Ah, there she comes again, running, and flushed and excited.

(*Truth runs up and throws herself at the feet of Experience.*)

Truth. Oh, protect me, you who look so wise and good. It was too horrible! How could they offer me to such a hideous ogre!

Exp. Don't be frightened, dear, you are safe here and can trust me. Calm yourself and tell us what has happened. That is right.

T. Well you saw how that horrid, wicked old Father of Lies took me in. When we got there it was quite dark, and I could make out neither the Absolute nor the Universal. But he stopped and cried out: 'Oh, Thou that art the Being of all beings, the Incomprehensible, the All-embracing, that wantest Nothing and hast Everything, lo, I present to Thee, Truth, the fair, the virgin, to have and to hold through all Eternity!' What right had he, I should like to know, to present me, seeing that I wasn't his to present?

Exp. You see you are so very presentable. And the Absolute, being utterly unpresentable, loves those like you, to absorb them.

T. The horror! But I must tell you what followed. Very soon after a hideous, shapeless, incomprehensible, intangible Something gathered round me. I could feel that It was trying to embrace me and nearly lost my senses. Still I struggled violently, but the cold, clammy, filthy Thing slobbered all over me. It was too disgusting for words. At last, in my despair, I drew out the sword with which I do up my hair, and stabbed at It furiously. Whether I killed It or not I do not know, but It relented. I got free, and managed to rush out as you saw.

Exp. My darling Truth, how brave, what a heroine you are! I see it all.

T. But can you understand it?

Exp. In a way, yes. It is when the Absolute is *absent-minded* that It behaves like that, or even worse. You see ordinarily It is both the Same and the Other, Self and Not-Self, Identity in Difference, through Difference, by, with and from Difference. It is Itself through not being Itself, and thereby returning to Itself reconciled with Itself. When It is like that It generally behaves Itself; at least the pholisophers say they can manage It. But when It is *absent-minded*, It is as it were *beside* Itself, and wholly Its Other (what the vulgar would call material), and then It thinks of nothing. Unfortunately this happens very often of late, indeed, almost constantly, and produces 'the absolute identity of absolute

Idealism and absolute Materialism'. Nevertheless the pholisophers defend Its 'going on the loose,' on the wretched plea that this is what It is etymologically bound to do, and that being thereby 'set loose,' It is more Absolute, more Itself: *i.e.*, such is Its intrinsic form of 'Self-realisation'. But even so, it seems very sad and bad. Especially as, even at the best of times, It is firmly convinced (by Bradley) that Morality is Appearance, and so not binding upon It. And when It thinks, It thinks so much of Itself that It always thinks that everybody is only too glad to be part of Itself. (*Truth*, indignantly, 'The idea!') and that It ought to embrace them. (*Truth*. 'Not me, thank you!') The Father of Lies of course knew all this and wanted you to be sacrificed, and absorbed by the Absolute, so as to become a mere *aspect* of It. But I am unspeakably glad that you have not only escaped from Its clutches, but helped others. For though you can hardly have killed It, you have certainly scotched it, and I fancy It will not readily recover. For the least resistance irritates It so much that it sets up a process of Self-diremption and disintegrates the lies which compose Its tissue. And the pholisophers also it will make so mad that they will become inarticulate, as well as unintelligible. And then, you know, it will be quite clear that they are no longer men, but either gods or beasts.

T. I am delighted to hear all this.

Exp. Come home then with me. We'll wash and have tea!

XXII.—THE INTERNATIONAL CONGRESS OF PHILOSOPHERS.

By the Joker.

Members of Congress.

The Pelican.[1]
The Joker.[1]
The Phœnix.[1]
The Sphinx.
The Wild Goose.
A Philosophic Night Mare.
A Duck's Egg.
The World Egg (Kosmosoon).
The Eozoon (of Canada).
The Autozoon (of Plato).
The Tyrannical Man (of Plato).
The Goat Stag (of Aristotle).
The Cock Horse (of Aristotle).
The Seal (of Solomon).
A Cygnet (of St. Johns).
The Leviathan (of Hobbes).
The Behemoth (of Hobbes).
The Ass (of Buridan).
The She-Ass (of Balaam).
The Serpent (of Eden).
The Serpent (of Eternity).
The Bull (of Shiva).
The Bull (of the Pope).
The Cow (of Isis).
The Absolute Cow (of Schelling).
The Squirrel (of Bradley).
A Herd of Chimeras (Bradley's).
The Chimera Bombinans (of Duns).
The Owl (of Hegel).
The Owlets (of Oldham).

[1] *Nullius addicti jurare in verba magistri.*

The First Vertebrate.
The Monera (of Haeckel).
The Bathybius (of Huxley).
The Pithecanthropus Erectus (of Dubois).
The Eagle (of Prometheus).
The Tortoise (of Achilles).
The Nile Crocodile (of Chrysippus).
The Mugger (of Kipling).
The Prize Pig (from the herd of Epicurus).
The Dog (befriended by Pythagoras).
The Dog (of Newton).
The Spider (of Bruce).
The Ant (of the Sluggard).
The Mallard Imaginaire (of All Souls).
The Salamander (of Paracelsus).
The Mock Turtle (of Carroll).
The Dodo (of Dodgson).
The Pigdog (*sui juris*).
The Bees (of Mandeville).
The Tree (of Porphyry).
The Pine (Fichte's).
The Lotus (of Buddha).
The Umbrella (of Kant) } for a rainy day.
The Wall (of Plato) }
Ursus Spelæus, the Cave-Bear.[1]

SCENE.—*The Happy Hunting Grounds, an open prairie plentifully sown with wild oats.*

The Joker. (*Aside.*) Do you suppose, Pelican, that the Cygnet really knows the way to the Congress?

The Pelican. Oh, yes, he knows all about Congresses.

The Cygnet. I fancy we shall find it round this corner.

Joker. Yes, here we are. What a queer lot they are! I apologise, Cygnet, for beginning to get anxious. You are a capital guide.

Pelican. Yes, and when he grows up he will make a capital swan. He is already quite stout.

Cygnet. I am glad there is such a good meeting. There must be nearly fifty present. But do you know any of them?

Pelican. I know them nearly all. Do you see that very owlish old owl, for instance, sitting on that ragged poplar-like tree yonder?

Cygnet. Yes.

Pelican. Well that is Hegel's Owl sitting on the Tree of

[1] *Alias*, Ed. of MIND!

Porphyry. It's no use going to talk to her, for whatever any one says she always hoots.

Cygnet. Why does she do that?

Pelican. Oh, she pretends to think nobody has done anything since Hegel mentioned her and made her famous, and nothing new or true has been said since. Let us rather talk to that eagle there. It's Prometheus' Eagle, who feeds daily on the vitals of Prometheus, but can't kill him. So he is a great authority on the mystery of suffering. Hallo! Eagle! Have you found Prometheus' vitals yet? or do you still treat them as victuals?

Joker. Could you oblige me with an answer to the riddle—What is life without the liver?

Eagle. No, the answer to that question concerns Prometheus, not me. All I do is to effect his daily delivery.

Pelican. Just let me stop that Wild Goose which is whizzing past. What's the matter, Goose? why be in such a hurry?

Goose. Oh, it's an awful business! They were chasing me as usual, and I was terribly upset and dropped my egg, and now I can't find it!

Pelican. (*Pointing to the World Egg.*) Why, what's this? Isn't this yours?

Goose. I do believe it is! Thank you ever so much, my dear Pelican. I can't think how you always manage to find things so cleverly in the most unlikely places! Now *I* should never have expected to find my poor egg at an International Congress of Philosophic Beasts. However, I'll sit down on it at once, else they'll be chasing me again, and I'll never get it hatched. (*Sits down.*)

Pelican. That's her monomania you know—she's always imagining herself 'chased'. But you'll see she won't sit on it long!

Joker. Hallo, here's the Fowler.

Pelican. Atrocious! What right has he to be here?

Joker. I suppose he is attracted by the quantity of rare birds he sees.

Pelican. I don't care, he shouldn't be allowed to scare us: it's very inconsiderate of the Committee!

Joker. Calm yourself, Pelican, it is not the Wild Fowler nor even the Warde Fowler; look at him!

Pelican. Oh, of course, it's the Tom Fowler, who is sure to be everywhere, and a very dear friend of mine! But why haven't you brought your beetles or stick-insects or whatever they call them to the Congress?

T. Fowler. Because I am no longer Vice-Chancellor and am enjoying myself.

The Wild Goose. Oh, I am sure I've been sitting on the wrong egg! What shall I do, Pelican? I feel certain that it's a Duck's Egg and nothing will ever come of it!

Pelican. Nonsense! The Duck's Egg is lying quietly in the Philosophic Night Mare's Nest over there. Sit still and don't worry us!

Joker. If you don't like one egg, try another, *i.e.* be *alter-eggoistic!*

Goose. I'm sure it's a bad egg! It's so cold and must be addled! Do come and look at it. (*Gets up.*)

Pelican. Well, it does look a little like the Curate's. But it may be good in parts.

Joker. Oh, blow it!

Pelican. Gracious no! It might explode!

Goose. They're after me again!

Joker. Who?

Goose. The pholisophers! I must fly! (*Flies off.*)

Cygnet to Pelican. Do you really think it is all only a delusion of hers?

Pelican. Hush! The Doctors of Pholisophy all say so, and I mustn't commit myself. Let us move on and look at the other freaks.

Joker. Well, tell us who they are. Is this great cobweb, for instance, supposed to be symbolic of philosophic thought?

Pelican. Oh, that has, I expect, been spun by Bruce's spider this morning.

Joker. How frightfully energetic! What does he expect to make by it?

Pelican. Oh, his great ambition is to catch a Behe-moth. But even if he doesn't, it keeps up his ethical reputation.

Joker. And what, pray, are those extraordinary creatures, assembled round that restless little squirrel in the cage?

Pelican. I think that must be part of Bradley's menagerie!

Cygnet. Yes, I recognise them. That is a herd of Assorted Chimeras. And the squirrel had to be shut up on account of its fierceness and lest it should grow too like the Absolute.[1] I dare say, if you look carefully, you will also find some of his theological, psychological and other monsters. I know all about them because I have introduced most of them to the British Public. I hear, however, he has got rid of his dog. They quarrelled about the reality of time. The dog's first principle was 'Whatever smells is real,' and Bradley could never convince him that thyme did not smell.

Joker. Are not all these monsters dangerous neighbours?

[1] Cp. *Appearance and Reality*, p. 172.

Pelican. Oh, you needn't be afraid! See how he has treated his chimeras and monsters. They are all pounded, cut, battered and slashed, and in no condition to hurt a fly. Besides they are only appearance.

Joker. How horrible! He seems to be a regular Dr. Moreau in his operations upon the creatures of his fancy! But why doesn't the Society for the Prevention of Cruelty to Philosophic Animals intervene.

Pelican. Oh, I suppose the mutilation also is Appearance. But here come the Owlets. Let us ask them what has been going on. Be welcome, Owlets, and come into my wings! Tell us what has happened so far.

1*st Owlet.* Oh, they began by reading a long letter of regret from Darwin's Missing Link, explaining that he could not come, because he could not find himself and so could not afford it, and denouncing the Pithecanthropus Erectus as an impostor. Then they had a difficulty with Jonah's Whale, who objected that the water in shore was so shallow that he feared to get stranded and wanted a special dock constructed that he might attend. So the extremists wanted to put him in the dock on a charge of *lèse-majesté*, but the Congress finally contented itself, though not him, with pointing out that Hobbes' Leviathan had raised no such difficulties. So now he is staying in the offing wailing. You can hear him when the Owl stops hooting.

Pelican. There are so many noises that it is hard to make out who produces what whence. And after that?

1*st Owlet.* Oh, they had a squabble about the credentials of the Tyrannical Man.

Pelican. Of course he could not be admitted to a Congress of Philosophic Beasts?

1*st Owlet.* Well, he quoted passages from his author to show that he was not only a beast, but many beasts.

2*nd Owlet.* And then by a revulsion of feeling they actually voted him into the chair!

3*rd Owlet.* I think that was really in order to render him helpless. For you know the Speaker hardly ever speaks.

1*st Owlet.* After that the Phœnix delivered an address on Purification by Fire and the Necessity of Re-Birth, which was generally regarded as quite unscientific and unworthy of the twentieth century.

Pelican. And what is going on now?

1*st Owlet.* If you hurry up you may hear the end of the Serpent's speech on the Future of Philosophy.

Joker. What Serpent is speaking? The Serpent of Eternity?

1st Owlet. No, that always wears its tail in its mouth, like a whiting, and so of course it can't speak. It's the Old Serpent of Eden, who can speak most persuasively.

Joker. Oh, we ought to hear him! But as we go, Pelican, would you mind just explaining to me why all you birds take such a leading part in the proceedings and seem to know all about everything?

Pelican. I suppose it is because we can fly and best find out which way the wind blows.

(*They reach the platform.*)

Serpent. . . . And now, Beasts of Philosophers, I have shown, in words, indeed, and more briefly than is demanded by the dignity of the subject, that the Future of Philosophy depends on the Future of Philosophers, and that the Future of Philosophers depends on their maintaining their proper obscurity. A philosopher understood, or capable of so being, is necessarily a philosopher misunderstood; for a philosopher understood rightly ceases to be such and to be esteemed as such. For a philosopher the sole commandment is the eleventh—'Don't be found out!' In it and by it all the rest are absorbed, transmuted and transcended. In philosophy levity is the destruction of gravity, brightness of insight, clearness of profundity. Let me beseech you therefore to shun the false goddess Lucidity, whom the vulgar ignorantly reverence, as you would the D——, I mean the Daily Male, and to cultivate with a whole-hearted unanimity the Unintelligibility to which you can all attain in words, even if you cannot in thought. And finally, to give practical effect to this recommendation, Beasts of Philosophers, let me move that henceforth the Absolute be substituted for the Deity, as the exclusive object of philosophic reverence, and that whosoever shall refuse after one year to fall down and worship It, shall be imprisoned and condemned to read the *Phenomenology of Absolute Nonsense* for life.

(*Great Sensation; even the Owl stops hooting.*)

The Autozoon. Beasts of Philosophers, in spite of the demoniac and almost Demosthenean eloquence of the last speaker, I move as an amendment that the whole body of philosophers be promoted to the world of Ideas, regardless of the public expense.

The Pelican to the Joker. As if they would go! That Autozoon is an incorrigible idealist! But at all events he is in favour of the Intelligible against the Unintelligible. For the Ideal world is in intelligible space (τόπος νοητός).

(*A great commotion, out of which the First Vertebrate slowly emerges.*)

The First Vertebrate. As the oldest, with the exception of my honourable friends the Bathybius, the Monera and the Eozoon, of those here assembled, as the ancestor certainly of the most prominent members of this distinguished company, may I be permitted to make a few remarks on this important question? (*Cries of Oh! No! Divide! The Owl hoots furiously.*) I see that you do not know who I am. You think I look a worm and am a worm. Well, you should not judge by appearances. I was a worm, but am a worm no longer. I have a *chorda dorsalis.* I am THE WORM THAT TURNED and so became a VERTEBRATE. Into the history of my struggles and my sufferings I will not enter. Suffice it to say that I felt the divine impetus to progress and at last made my way out of my native obscurity, and if not yet beautiful, I am yet suggestive. I therefore strongly deprecate any return to obscurity of any kind. Should you however decide in favour of darkness, I solemnly warn you, *I shall turn again!* I shall become a *Revertebrate,* and on my return the universal process of Cosmic Dissolution and Degeneration foreshadowed by Spencer must necessarily ensue!

(*Indescribable sensation. The Owl hoots.*)

Autozoon. I rise to withdraw my amendment. It appears that we are not unanimous. I cannot understand it at all. For we ought to be unanimous and united. I object to the harsh measures proposed by the Serpent, and am confident that if we only knew each other better and met more frequently all differences could be reconciled. (*Great applause. The Owl hoots.*) But I confess I hardly see what measures should be taken.

Pelican. Beasts of Philosophers, before we can be reconciled, must we not first of all find out what are the various views that have to be reconciled? (*Hear! hear! The Owl hoots.*) I propose therefore the appointment of a Committee of Inquiry into the State of Philosophic Sentiment, with a view to ascertaining what possibilities of agreement exist. And secondly I demand a show of paws and claws on the motion of the Serpent. (*To Joker.*) That, I think, will dish the Serpent! He has neither!

(*The Tyrannical Man puts the question, and after a pause declares that on a show of paws the Serpent's motion is rejected by* 48 *to* 3, *and the Pelican's carried.*)

Serpent. In order to show my acquiescence in the sentiment of the Congress I propose that the Pelican and the Joker be appointed to the Committee of Inquiry with power to add to their number. They are, I fancy, well versed in inquiries into the eccentricities of sentiment.

(*Carried by acclamation. The Owl still hoots.*)

Pelican. He thinks he has inflicted the devil of a job on us. But we'll beat him yet! Come along and let us collect some representative opinions from those who have not yet said anything.

Joker. All right. Let us ask this very emaciated donkey. He looks extremely representative.

Pelican. What! Buridan's Ass? It's no use asking him. He can't make up his mind even to eat his hay. That is why he is so thin.

Joker. Then let us listen to that Lotus. I have never yet heard a flower that could talk, and what it says might be interesting.

The Lotus. Om mane padme hum.

Pelican. How do you think, Lotus, we can best secure the future of Philosophy and the agreement of Philosophers?

Lotus. Om mane padme hum.

Joker. Is that all? Say it again slowly!

Lotus. Om—mane—padme—hum.

Pelican. Come away, Joker, and leave it to *om mane padme hum.* It's an automaton and can say nothing else. Let us rather ask the Sphinx who has sat silent and looked wise all this time. Sphinx, wake up! Whose are you, Œdipus'? or an Egyptian?

Sphinx. No, Schiller's.

Pelican. All the better, tell us what you think.

Sphinx. I have many things in and on my MIND! Let us appeal to the British public and publish them!

Joker. Bravo, Sphinx! That is the solution. You alone of us all seem to be *Compos Mentis!*

(*Exeunt omnes, except the Owl, left hooting, and Duns' Chimera, left 'buzzing in the void'.*)

XXIII.—NURSERY RHYMES FOR PHILOSOPHIC BEGINNERS.

1.—*Pretty MIND!*

"Where are you going to, my pretty MIND!?"
"I'm going a-begging just now, Sir, I find."
"And whom will you beg from, my pretty MIND!?"
"Whoever is witty, Sir, whom I can find."
"And where will you find any, my pretty MIND!?"
"Wherever the eyes, Sir, of people aren't blind."
"Can I be of help to you, my pretty MIND!?"
"I think so. To help me I'm sure you are kind!"

2.

Little Jack Horner sat in a corner,
Reading his Christmas MIND!
When to jokes he would come, he'd pull out the plum
And say, "'Tis a capital find!"

3.—*Nova Mentis!* 1901.

Twinkle, twinkle, Little Star,
Won't they wonder what you are?
Up above the fogs so high,
How they'll hate you till they die!

4.—*Pretty MIND! again.*

"Where are you going to, my pretty MIND!?"
"I'm going to puzzle some folks, Sir, I find."
"And how will you puzzle them, my pretty MIND!?"
"By laughing at folly of every kind."
"And why will you puzzle them, my pretty MIND!?"
"Because, Sir, pholisophy funny I find."
"But think you this profits us, my pretty MIND!?"
"I hope, Sir, to open the eyes of the blind."
"But that were a miracle, my pretty MIND!?"
"Ah, but my jokes, Sir, are wondrous refined."

5.—*The Hen and the Pan.*

Muddily, Maddily, Men,
The Pan has swallowed the Hen!
Maddily, Muddily, Man,
The Hen has jumped from the Pan!

6.—*῞Εν καὶ Πᾶν.*

Humpty D—— was the Great All,
Humpty D—— had a great fall,
Not all the Hen's asses, nor all the Pan's men
Shall put that old incubus on us again!

7.—*Great Πᾶν.*

Great Pan is dead,
There's little to be said:
Had it been his father,[1]
I would much rather;
Had it been his Other,
One's joy one could smother;
But now it is Pan,
You're free again, Man!

8.

I do not like you, Dr. Fell,
The reason why I'd like to tell;
But after all it's just as well,
I cannot tell you, Dr. Fell.

9.—*Reason and Feeling.*

Said Twaddledum to Twaddledee—
"I'm sure that you'll agree with me!"
Said Twaddledee to Twaddledum—
"I cannot help it, I am dumb!"

10.—*The One.*

There was an old Owl who lived in a Shoo!
Annoyed by the Many who at her would boo,
She gave them some Hegel without any bread,
And whipped them all soundly and put them to bed.

[1] "Whom do you mean? The father of Pantheism?"—Ed., Mind! "Of Lies."—Author.

11.—*Mr. Bradley's Postulate.*[1]

If 'musts' and 'cans'
Were Hens and Pans
There'd be no need for thinkers!

12.—*Three Blind Mice.*

Three Blind Mice, see how they run!
They all run after the B——'s hoax,
Who quickly in action their interest chokes,
And cuts off their power to see any jokes!
Three blind mice!

13.

Old Mother Hegel
Tried to inveigle
A poor god into her home;
But when he came there
She stripped him quite bare—
So this is the end of the pome!

14.—*Τὸ Μὴ Ὄν.*

There is an abstraction called Nothing-at-all,
Concerning which pholisophs terribly pall:
If Something be Nothing, and Nothing be All,
Then what is the Meaning of Nothing-at-all?

15.

Hey diddle diddles
The Sphinx and her Riddles!
The Owlets no answer could find,
The Pelican smiled to see them so wild
And printed the answers in MIND!

[1] Usually formulated as '*What must be and can be, that therefore is*'.

XXIV.—THE WELBY PRIZE.

LADY WELBY, whose interest in clearing up intellectual fogs and purifying the philosophical atmosphere is well known, has offered a prize of £1,000 to any philosopher who can produce adequate documentary evidence to show that he

(1) Knows what he means.
(2) ,, ,, any one else ,,
(3) ,, ,, every one ,,
(4) ,, ,, anything ,,
(5) ,, ,, everything else ,,
(6) Means what he says.
(7) ,, ,, ,, means.
(8) ,, ,, every one else ,,
(9) ,, ,, ,, ,, says that he means.
(10) Can express what he means.
(11) Knows what it signifies what he means.
(12) ,, ,, it matters ,, ,, signifies.

At first sight it might seem as though the Twelve Labours of Hercules would be in comparison with this a slighter achievement. But in view of the extensive and peculiar knowledge of the Absolute's Mind which is now possessed by so many philosophers, a large number of solutions may confidently be expected. These should be sent in to the Editors of MIND! Corpus Christi College, Oxford, *before the issue of the next number.*

XXV.—CRITICAL NOTICES.

Ἀναξιμάνδρου περὶ φύσεως. Erste vollständige Ausgabe. Von Prof. Dr. PRELLER.

THE name of the supposed author of this curious work, M. Anaximandros of Miletos, is new to science, and but for the sponsorship of so well-known a savant as Dr. Preller, one would be inclined to suspect a hoax. As it is, it may charitably be supposed that M. Anaximandros was an autodidact. He appears to have been a man of great ingenuity and varied scientific interests, if, as appears from Dr. Preller's learned introduction, he set up sundials at Sparta, calculated the perimeter of the earth, cast horoscopes, and tamed Sciotheres. Nevertheless we can not agree that this sumptuous collection of his papers was at all called for. Scientifically it is not too much to say that what is true in them is Darwinian and what is new in them is unsound or unintelligible. And unfortunately, M. Anaximandros corrupts what science he possesses by an obscure and gratuitous metaphysic. He regards all things as differentiations of the Infinite (for so it would seem we must translate his *Ἄπειρον*, though it is by no means clear whether it is a mathematical or material infinite or the undefined matrix of elementary evolution). But what is the use of so vague a principle?

Coming to biology, we note that M. Anaximandros is a thorough-going evolutionist, who adopts a number of Darwinian doctrines. He holds that organic life originated in the water, and that the hard chitinous and calcareous coats and spines of primitive fishes, crustacea and insects were protective. In his ingenious and well-reasoned argument, that man must have been evolved out of the lower animals, on account of the prolongation of his helpless infancy, which would otherwise have proved fatal to the survival of the nascent human race, he seems to be unaware that he has been anticipated by Prof. Fiske some time ago. Nevertheless it must be admitted that he appears to have reached all these results independently, and though he tells us little about them, it is evident that he has made prolonged and careful observations. As an exhibition of scientific enterprise and interest on the bigoted and barbarous coast of Asia Minor M. Anaximandros' work deserves a word of praise.

O. T. Poultison.

Aristokles: περὶ πολιτείας.

We had hoped to present our readers with an exhaustive criticism of this important work, by one who is undoubtedly the most competent and trustworthy authority on the true Socratic doctrine, *viz.*, Lieut.-Gen. X. N. O'Fun, V.C., F.R.G.S., etc., but just as we were going to press we received from him the following message by wireless telepathy.

"Profoundly regret cannot send 'Critical Notice' of Plato's book. Owing to strikes, stock of asbestos paper run out. Industrial revolution imminent. Infernal nuisance. Just off on Antarctic expedition. Never Mind! or say die!"

In spite of this disappointment we have managed to secure what should interest our readers, *viz.*, an authentic and contemporaneous advertisement, giving an excellent idea of the way in which the *Republic* was received by the Press on its first appearance.

A New and Important Work on Philosophy.

Περὶ Πολιτείας.

By

Aristokles, the Son of Ariston, LL.D.

Perpetual President of the Athenian Academy, Hon. Member of the College of Nomothetæ, Officer of the Laconian Legion of Honour, etc.

Extracts from Press notices:—

Nus says: "Will undoubtedly be widely read and excite much controversy, but is too extravagant to live".

Physis: "Its science is crude, but its advocacy of Artificial Selection should prove interesting to biologists".

Theates: "Its tone is admirable, and we enjoyed the first and last books immensely. The central books can hardly be meant to be taken seriously."

Laconist: "Every patriotic Laconian should read it. The Ideal State is practically ours."

Agora Howler: "A venomous display of aristocratic rancour, whose author should be prosecuted under the γραμμὴ παραγραφῶν".

Phylax: "Treasonable enough to put a severe strain on our traditional policy of the utmost literary toleration".

N.B., *The Chronoi* are giving away a copy to each purchaser of their Athenian Encyclopædia.

Studies in the Hooligan Dialectic. By J. E. M. TAGRAG. Pp. 259.

MR. TAGRAG is an enthusiastic admirer of the Hooligan Dialectic, which he regards as the method destined to reform Logic and revolutionise Philosophy. We confess that these hopes of Mr. Tagrag's seem to us somewhat sanguine, not to say sanguinary, and cannot find in the Hooligan Dialectic much beyond a systematisation of the old *Argumentum Baculinum,* for which arm-chair philosophers have always expressed their contempt with impunity. Nevertheless by his very full and curious account of the methods of "mafficking" Mr. Tagrag has deserved well of Science, while his lucid discussion of the difficult problem (p. 139) of whether a girl subjected to the osculatory attentions of a promiscuous crowd acquires more cheek or less cheek, is delightfully luminous and convincing. On the whole we have to thank Mr. Tagrag for an interesting volume which no serious social philosopher can afford to ignore.

A. CAVEY.

URSUS SPELÆUS, M.A., *More Riddles from Worse Sphinxes.*

WHEN our colleague and friend the Editor of *Mind* volunteered to contribute to our pages a review of this epoch-making work, we naturally thanked him, and regarded the matter as settled. Hence it was no slight shock to be informed by our trusty reviewer, shortly before going to press, that after using all known methods, including the extraction of the Infinite Root, he had found the Riddles insoluble, and the Sphinxes indomitable. Fortunately a happy thought soon struck us (in the frontal region). We remembered that our Office Boy had severely sprained his ankle, in his anxiety to imitate the barbarous manners of his Troglodyte ancestors, and so happened to be well qualified for the *rôle* of Œdipus. We at once put him on half-pay and set him the following Conundrums to guess:—

1. Why did Ingram Bywater?
2. Why was Bacon bought?
3. When does B—— bawl?
4. Why did B—— burn it?
5. Whom did L—— love?
6. Why can't the Baldwin?
7. When is Keats Keats?
8. Why was B—— blunt?
9. Why did S—— sully?
10. What did Carveth Read?
11. Why did B—— bustle?
12. Why was M—— married?
13. Why did Suleika?

Our confidence was not deceived. In due course we were provided with the subjoined replies, whose relevance may be conjectured:—

1. Because he could not buy Stout.
2. Because there was a Bidder.
3. When K—— Knocks.
4. Because he couldn't Locke it.
5. A Nietzsche.
6. Because Kant couldn't.
7. When he isn't Keatinge.
8. Because W—— was wily.
9. Because he was to Grose.
10. Mere Cormorant.
11. Because nobody Cared.
12. Because he went to Kirk.
13. Because she did not know Joseph (Yussuf).

If, after that, any one wants *Worse Riddles from More Sphinxes*, we pity him!

ED., MIND!

XXVI.—NOTES AND NEWS.

We cull the following from the *Ecclesia Guardian* (Φύλαξ ἐκκλησίας) of 1st April, 399 B.C. :—

" We have to announce to-day the lǒng-expected death last night of a well-known character of old Athens, Sōkrates the son of Sophroniskos, of the deme Alopeke. All who knew 'old Soak' (and who did *not?*) will not be surprised to learn that death occurred somewhat suddenly, in consequence of his drinking something which disagreed with him. Much sympathy is expressed for his hard-working and highly respected wife, Xanthippe, and her young family, who are left quite unprovided for and will probably come upon the second half of her husband's name."

The *Theates* remarks :—

" The literary world has been greatly excited by the death of Sokrates. It is rumoured that many of our best-known men of letters, including Aristokles, the son of Ariston, and Xenophon, the son of Gryllos, are already engaged upon biographies of the defunct celebrity, which are confidently expected to mark an era in the history of philosophy."

In a later issue the *Ecclesia Guardian* says :—

" It is with considerable reluctance that we are compelled to return to the distasteful subject of the death of Sokrates, the son of Sophroniskos. But, presumably on the principle that any stick is good enough to beat a dog with, a most extraordinary legend has been constructed about this event by the aristocratic literary clique whose rancorous hatred of democratic institutions appears to shrink from no excess of falsehood and absurdity. Our correspondent in Syracuse writes to us in great concern, to know whether it is true, as he has been positively informed, that Sokrates was condemned by the dicastery and compelled to drink the hemlock, on a (really political) charge of impiety. Now, of course, every one in Athens knows that *hemlock* was not the favourite poison of poor 'old Soak' and that the cause of his death is far more likely to have been *absinthe,* but in order to check the circulation of such falsehoods it may be well to state the exact facts. The report of the Superintendent of Police shows that the alleged victim of democratic spite was found, on the night of the 20th of Elaphebolion last, lying unconscious on the steps of the Prytaneum, and taken to the lock-up. The police surgeon diagnosed the case by smell and in accordance with the known character of the deceased as syncope, but has since admitted that at his age the immediate cause of death may have been an apoplectic seizure. The patient never recovered consciousness, and died at daybreak in the prison, a fact which seems to be the only element of truth in the monstrous fictions which have been circulated."

Students of philosophy will have been greatly concerned to hear of the death of Empedokles, the discoverer of the Elements, of the Great Law of Universal Polarity and of the Rhythm of Evolution and Dissolution. As various painful and absurd rumours have been circulated with regard to the circumstances of his death, we quote the following authentic account of the accident from *Physis* of the 10th of Boedromion, 428 B.C. :—

"It is with great regret that we record the sad death of Dr. Empedokles, the best-known citizen of Akragas. Dr. Empedokles, whose attainments were equally remarkable as a physician, philosopher, poet and statesman, was accustomed to spend his summer vacation in the scientific exploration of his native island, and it appears from the *Syracuse Herald* that it was on one of these expeditions that he fell a victim to his scientific zeal. He had set out with a small but well-equipped party to ascend Mount Ætna, with a view to making seismological observations on the summit. The ascent was successfully achieved, but Dr. Empedokles' scientific ardour subsequently induced him to attempt to explore the crater. He had descended about a hundred feet, when he suddenly fell, overpowered apparently by the sulphurous fumes issuing from the volcano. The body could not be recovered, but at, great risk of his life, his assistant secured one of his sandals which had fallen off on to a projecting rock It has been deposited in the temple of Apollo at Akragas."

We regret to state that Hegeloiosis (ἡ γελοιωσις) is still rampant in certain philosophic circles. The Doctors of Philosophy appear to be quite incapable of coping with the ravages of this insidious disease, which, originally made (for export only) in Germany, has now assumed the proportions of a cachinnational danger.

We hear Prof. * * * has *espoused* the cause of the Absolute. It is rumoured that Mrs. * * * was about to sue for a divorce on the ground of bigamy, but was advised that the courts would probably hold that the Absolute had no cause.

MIND! is *not* going to be substituted for Bacon in the Honour School of *Lit. Hum.* It is asserted, however, that the Board of Faculty saved its bacon by a narrow majority.

XXVII.—NEW BOOKS.

Sense and Sensibility. By JANE AUSTEN.

[IT is we believe in a romance of Jean Paul Richter's that two young people, a brother and sister, are described as being too poor to buy books, but as making amends for the deficiency by composing books for themselves, to suit the titles of those they saw advertised. It occasionally happens that a reviewer, as short of time as this ingenious pair were of money, has recourse to a somewhat similar method, constructs the book, that is, from its title, and criticises it accordingly—with results of a sometimes rather startling character, as the following extracts from three representative organs of European opinion may serve to show.]

"Verfasserin dieses Werkes ist die berühmte, von Macaulay als Vermittlerin zwischen Deutschland und England neben Shakspeare hochgepriesene Feministin Jane Austen, die schon in ihrer wertvollen kulturhistorischen Arbeit *Pride and Prejudice* gegen die engherzigen Vorurteile und den anmassenden Stolz der englischen aristokratisch-hochkirchlichen Gesellschaft einen kräftigen Stoss geführt hat, während sie gleichzeitig als Dichterin der *Persuasion* gegen die Zwangsehe und für die Rechte der freien Liebe mutvoll aufgetreten ist. In der vorliegenden Abhandlung sucht die beredte Vorkämpferin ihres Geschlechtes der Wurzel des Uebels näher zu treten indem sie durch eine Reihe der scharfsinnigten Analysen die feinsten Fasern des weiblichen Empfindungsvermögens bloss legt, und endlich siegreich bis zu einer rein monistischen, bzw. materialistischen, alle Dissonanzen verwischenden und alle Gegensätze versöhnenden, Weltanschauung durchdringt. Wir begrüssen dieses treffliche Buch als ein erfreuliches Zeichen dass auch auf brittischen Boden, wo Recht und Wahrheit sonst am spätesten über die Bewusstseinsschwelle zu steigen pflegen, endlich die Morgenröte der Frauenemanzipation anhebt."—*Moria Roth im "Maulwurf"*.

"M. Lombroso nie la sensibilité chez les femmes. Mlle Austen affirme au contraire dans sa qualité de femme qu'elles sentent parfaitement bien, et même que la sensibilité est un petit signe particulier que la nature leur a donné en propre. Voilà un assez joli débat engagé. Lequel des deux a tort, lequel des deux a raison? Nous laissons volontiers la réponse a nos lecteurs et surtout à Mesdames nos lectrices."—*La Nuit Noire.*

"Miss Jane Austen is, we believe, a sister of Miss Sarah Austen, the well-known author of *Pride and Prejudice*, and nearly connected with the Poet Laureate. The name of the family is a guarantee for sound workmanship. . . . Miss Austen is not one of those who fancy that human aspirations can be measured by an electrometer."—*The Garden Critic.*

The Cardinal and His Conscience. By ETERNAL HOPE.

As might have been expected, the ill-assorted couple are soon parted. The *How* should be read, to understand the *Why*. The author differs from Mr. Bradley in esteeming the *What* above the *That*, and maintaining the transcendent importance of knowing *What's what* in the *Here* and *Now*.

TWITTAKER.

BOOKS RECEIVED.

We hope to do justice, or more, to the following publications in subsequent issues.

Posthumous Selections from the Good Intentions (First and Second) of Philosophy Professors. Edited by A. LUCKY CHANCE and published by the Hades Publishing Co., *Edition de luxe*, on asbestos paper, £5 5s.

The Psychological Baby. Its Care and Cure. Authorised translation from the American of Dr. KINDERSPOTT, Professor of Pædology in the Washbosh Abnormal School, Wis.

Der Halbweltschmerz. Seine Bedeutung und seine Behandlung. Von Kurarzt Dr. BLUNDER.

Types of Ethical Theorists. Illustrated by F. GARROTTERS GOULD. 2 vols.

The Will to Deceive. By Dr. JIMJAMS.

More Hegelisms from Worse Hashish. By BILJAMES EFFENDI.

The Spirit of Modern Frivolity. By Prof. R. E. JOYCE.

A Treatise of Inhuman Nature. By DAVID X. HUME.

A Butler's Apology. By A. SILVER SPOONER.

An Emetic Psychology. By TARTAR E. METIQUE.

The Hypo-Critical Philosophy of Cant. 3 vols. Translated by Sir TAINE NIGHT-MARE, Kt.
Braddlenstein and His Monsters. By RITA.
On the Misinterpretation of the Nondescriptures. By Prebendary TWADLER.
Drinking, Billing and Cooing. By E. W. ANGELL, Ph.D.
The Progress of Moral Disorder. By SALLY MANDER.
The Problem of Misconduct. A Study of Infant Phenomenology. By A. NAYLOR.
The Future of Geloiocracy. By DE TOQUÉ VILLE.
The Syntax of Sense. By the Author of the *Grammar of Science.*
Time and Trouble. A key to the *Philosophy of Reflection.* By A METAPHYSICIAN OF EXPERIENCE.
Instinct with Reason. By H. RUTGERS, Marshal of the U.S. A(rmy).
Modern Psychopompology. By HEBE KITCHENER, M.A., Ph.D.
A Bare Outline of Psychopompology. By the Same.
The Voyage of the Othere. By the Same.
A Handbook of Practical Geloiology. By A. SCOFFINGHOUR.
Paralelogismena and Perierga. By the Same.
The Secret of MIND! By A. POUND STERLING.
Talks to Preachers. By the Author of *Side Talks to Girls.*
The Theory and Practice of Ignorance. By A. CRICHTON, Professor of Metanoiology and Physametics in the Sage and Onions School of Pholisophy. Troy Town, N.J.[1]
Informal Logic. For Ladies. By ANNA LODGICK, Sc.D.
The Elements of Analogic. An Autobiography. By A. LODGICK, Sc.D.
Outlines of Comic Pholisophy. By JOHN FRISKE, LL.D.
Social Ecstatics. By HERBERT MACKINTOSH.
Lectures on Human and Animal Pedagogy. By A. WOODD VEDDAH.
Some Emotions and a Pill. By A. PAIN.
Plain Truths about the Absolute. 1d. (2d. Coloured).
The Good Hegelian and the Bad Infinite. An Ethical Dialogue for Sunday Schools. By JOE KING, D.D.
Advice to an Ingenuous Youth about to Study Pholisophy. By An ASTUTER.
Attempts at Degrees of Truth. For the use of Candidates. Universe Extension Handbooks, No. 1.
Prometheus. Unbound in Paper Covers. By P. B. SHELLY, 1st edition.

[1] N.J. = Not, apparently, *New Jersey*, but *No Joke.*

The Double Eagle and the Gold Standard. A plea for Ornitheology *versus* Capitalism. By W. J. PRIAM.

The Philosophy of the Unconscionable. By E. von MANNHARDT.

The Squirm Spasm. A Theory of Absurdity. By Prof. JOACHIM JONES.

The Origin Series, I., *The Origin of Genus,* II., *The Origin of Specie.* By C. STARWIN. [*The Origins of Deference, Property* and *Accidents* to appear shortly.]

XXVIII.—ANSWERS TO CORRESPONDENTS.

COLNEY HATCHED CHICKEN.—If you have lost your *Mind*, get another from Messrs. Williams & Norgate.

WOULD-BE MIND ! READER.—Of course you can try Telepathy, but we expect a postal order would be more satisfactory.

MULTIPERPLEXED PERSONALITY.—If you have lost your Sympathetic Unity of Apperception, put yourself in a doctor's hands at once. The police are practically useless in such cases.

TUTOR.—Your symptoms indicate incipient fossilisation of the cortex. You should try the MIND ! cure.

MATERIALIST.—If you think MIND ! does not exist, call at our office (without your revolver) any morning between ten and one.

INDIGNANT OPTIMIST.—It seems very unfair. You had better inquire of the Eternal Cussedness.

PESSIMIST.—If life is not worth living, you might try whether death is worth dying.

PLATONIST.—No ; we did not notice any new Ideas at the Universal Exposition. The Idea of the Beautiful was *très chic et très Parisienne :* the Idea of Truth just a little overdressed.

INQUIRER.—Consult our back numbers for new *Weltanschauungen.* You should find no difficulty in disposing of your last 2nd-hand. Second-hand *Weltanschauungen* are usually firmly held, and realise good prices at auctions.

SPECULATIVE PHILOSOPHER.—(1) The *Hades Exploration Co.* is a sound undertaking with immense possibilities. Its management has not always been good, but you had better hold your shares for a rise. (2) The *Fairbairn Pastoral Co.* is an investment you are likely to do well by holding. (3) *The Absolute Ego Mine* seems to us greatly over-capitalised and we do not see how you can receive any returns. Moreover its promoters have not hitherto been fortunate in their undertakings.

Ἡγελαστη.—You have our entire sympathy. It was mere carping 'Sidgwickedness,' which is best disregarded. It is outrageous to be asked to change the convictions of a lifetime merely because they finally land one in contradictions. Do not, therefore, on meeting such, yield to the cruel and cowardly 'instinct of trying to get rid of them'. As for 'distinguishing between the contradictions which are evidence of error and those which are intimations of a higher truth,' why not adhere firmly to the simple rule that the former are *those of others*, the latter *your own?* In this way you simply *cannot go wrong*, or at least cannot be *convicted* of having done so.

ARISTOPHANES.—We regret that we cannot publish your contribution. Some respect must be shown to the elementary canons of decency even in flattering the Absolute.

HERETIC.—We dare not publish your amusing but paradoxical paper, *Why should Philosophy be dull?* at present. As for Philosophers, there is no reason why they should be dull in future, if they will only read and support MIND! assiduously.

FOURTH YEAR MAN.—(1) A little rhubarb and more physical exercise should be beneficial. (2) Ask your doctor as to what is the proper regimen 'for the Schools'. (3) Your tutor probably knows what he is about in recommending "*Aperients and Diareality*". (4) We do not agree that "morality is appearance" and that it is "impossible for a philosopher to *save Appearances*".

SCIPIO PUBLICANUS.—We greatly like your method of establishing the spirituous nature of the Absolute by showing that it is "above proof," and agree that it constitutes a distinct advance on Hegel's. It is certainly shorter. We hope to publish your paper in a subsequent issue.

PERPLEXED KANTIAN.—We are glad to be able to assure you that the Mystery of the Categorical Imperative has at length been solved. It is neither more nor less than MIND! With its contents you should lose no occasion to render yourself familiar. You will find thrice as many *really necessary truths* on a page of MIND! as in a volume of Kant or Hegel.

WANTED, for the purposes of Science, a GENTLEMAN who would be willing to devote himself to a life of absolute EGOISM. References to reputable moralists given and required. Apply to DIRECTOR of Moral Experiment Station, Exeter.

WANTED IMMEDIATELY, for Teaching Purposes, an INTELLIGIBLE ABSOLUTE. Money no object. Apply to "Tutor," c/o Ed., MIND!

WANTED TO EXCHANGE (owing to former owner's retirement from business) a pair of GREEN PARROTS (in Cairdboard Cages). Guaranteed to talk. A Hen- and Pan-coop would be accepted in exchange. "Novus Homo," c/o Ed., MIND!

WANTED an ANCILLARY PHILOSOPHY. Good Wages. Comfortable home. "Theologia," Keble.

FOR SALE a number of CATEGORICAL IMPERATIVES: for use on the Tow-path. "Moralist," c/o Ed., MIND!

A CULTURED and Refined HOME for DECAYED SHIBBOLETHS is offered by a married Tutor of an ancient College in one of our oldest universities. Terms moderate and inclusive. "Senex," c/o Ed., MIND!

LECTURE JOKES AND CATCHWORDS! Supplied by the MIND! Publishing Co. Fit guaranteed at first hearing. Send for our price list. The well-known Ex-President of the O.U.A.C., Achilles Thetisson, writes :—

> "Thanks to your new CATCHWORDS I have at last overtaken the *Tortoise* (with the utmost ease), and have consequently had my 'Blue' restored to me. It is a great relief to be no longer a paralogism, and I feel that I owe my athletic rehabilitation entirely to you."

ALL EXAMS prepared for by our *New Methods. Hypnotic Coaching, Mind! Reading, Suggestions, Clairvoyance, Prophecy.* SUCCESS ASSURED. Our travellers regularly visit all the Examiners and by MIND! READING ascertain their intentions. The Scholastic Preparation Syndicate, Oxford.

FOR SALE by Private Treaty. A UNIQUE MS., recently discovered in Egypt, of HEROTTIDUS, BOOK X., containing his account of the HYPERATLANTEANS, their Manners, Customs, Philosophy, etc. Collectors of Americana please note.

SELF-REALISATION (Unlimited) in Bankruptcy. The Official Receiver will register the claims of the credulous against this concern. They may be proved up to the 31st of December.

THE NATIONAL HOME FOR BACKWARD AND REFRACTORY PARENTS,

UNDER ROYAL AND IMPERIAL PATRONAGE,

Founded and Endowed by Andrew Carnegie,

IS NOW OPEN.

SALUBRIOUSLY situated at Homestead, Pa. Spiritual Illumination and every modern comfort and attention. Instruction in Amiability, Modernity, Nomenclature, the Logic of Relatives and of Events, etc. Terms inclusive. Write for descriptive pamphlet to MANAGER.

A DISTINGUISHED CRANKOLOGIST

Is prepared to give lessons in this important subject.

'Crankology has now become indispensable in education and politics.'

Apply to S.T.P., c/o Ed., MIND!

THE ONLY PHILOSOPHY THAT PAYS!!!

MONEYISM!

Why waste Labour and Money on Difficult and Expensive Brands, when OURS is the CHEAPEST and EASIEST?

SPECULATION MADE INFALLIBLE

By our Moneyist Principles.

Read *The Open Mind* and send for our Pamphlets: *How to Speculate, How I Found Out the Absolute, The Secret of the Universe in One Shot*, etc.

The MONEYIST PUBLISHING CO., 666 Dearbought St., Chicago, Ill.

When you go to Oxford

Don't omit to Visit

THE DIALECTICAL SYNOPTICON,

WITH ITS

Superb Series of Dissolving Weltanschauungen.

By Permission of the Vice-Chancellor and the Proctors, daily throughout Term Time.

LEE'S PATENT ANTI-FAD.

TRY IT! TRY IT!! TRY IT!!!

For the Church, the Army and Navy, and all the Learned Professions.

Prof. X., F.R.S., etc., writes: "Since taking ONE BOTTLE I have given up ALL MY MOST CHERISHED CONVICTIONS!"

Messrs. *JUGGINS & CO.*

Have great pleasure in announcing that they have

Just Received from Germany

A FINE CONSIGNMENT OF ASSORTED WELTANSCHAUUNGEN.

GOOD FOR THE SCHOOLS!!!

A First in LIT. HUM. writes: "Your latest 'Immoralist' WELTANSCHAUUNG was a great success. It was showy and wears well. It quite paralysed the Examiners, who proved utterly incapable of coping with and even of understanding it. Please send me another for the Civil Service Exam. A cheap one with plenty of facts and few ideas will do."

THE DICTIONARY OF OXFORD MYTHOLOGY.

Containing a complete historical account of the stories commonly told, and the men to whom they have from time to time been attached. For the use of Senior and Junior Common Rooms. By a Committee of Graduates and Undergraduates. Clarendon Press, N.D. 6 vols. 8vo.

UNEXPURGATED EDITION, £10 10s.

A genial Don writes:—

"I have found your Dictionary simply invaluable in arresting the flow of anecdotage in Common Room. An exact reference to the authoritative form of every story any one attempted to tell has invariably quenched the teller. If, as I should suppose, other Colleges contain *the men* to pursue a similar policy, your Dictionary will undoubtedly work a SOCIAL REVOLUTION in Oxford. In my own Common Room rational conversation has once more become possible (though not yet actual)."

A Balliol Scholar writes:—

"We tried one night to find stories you had omitted, and to invent fresh ones about the foibles of our dons. The fact that we failed egregiously in both cases conclusively establishes the COMPLETENESS of your Dictionary."

An American Mother writes:—

"*So* interesting. We are studying it in the *Chatauqua Home Reading Circles* this winter, and it is making Culture hum all over the West. I now feel that I quite understand the Oxford University life which puzzled us so much last summer."

R450034 UNKNOWN 091990

MIND

9911 OR ZKRR 5 98200 06

DD-3700